Praise for
THE HEROIC PATH

"John is a loyal friend, husband, and dad, and his book is witty, honest, and full of heart. I'm excited for you to get to know him."
—Kelly Clarkson

"I'm part of a generation of 'lost boys' that have a growing desire to somehow brave the transition out of Neverland and into the true epic—the life of a good man. John bids us to follow as he claws his way to the heart of manhood."
—Josh Garrels, singer and songwriter

"I love the way John sifts through the mixed and unhelpful messaging about what it means to be a man. In these beautifully written pages, he's searching for more than hammers and guns, and instead recovering qualities like honor, fidelity, and strength. This is important work."
—Shauna Niequist, author of *Bread & Wine*

"This book is an awakening for those who realize men have lost their way and are looking for something deeper—something *mythic*. This is not your everyday 'bravado man' book—this is *Fight Club* for intellectuals."
—Claire Díaz-Ortiz, head of social innovation, Twitter

"THE HEROIC PATH takes you off the grid into the deep woods to see things you've never seen before. You will not return the same."   —Ed Eason, lead guitarist for Carrie Underwood

"I have a great appreciation for John Sowers, his words, his self-deprecating wit, and for his huge heart for the fatherless generation. In THE HEROIC PATH, John weaves together all three so men might feel a little less daunted about the road that lies ahead."

—Lindsey Nobles, Director of Speakers, Conferences, and Social Media Fundraising at Feed the Children

"If you want a mundane life, throw this book down immediately and go seek shelter. But if you are hunting for the wild masculine, read on. This book is not an instruction manual; it is a soul insurrection."

—Jon Collins, digital storyteller at Sincerely Truman

THE
HEROIC
PATH

Also by John Sowers

Fatherless Generation: Redeeming the Story

THE HEROIC PATH

IN SEARCH OF THE MASCULINE HEART

JOHN SOWERS

JERICHO
BOOKS

New York   Boston   Nashville

Jericho Books
Hachette Book Group
237 Park Avenue
New York, NY 10017
www.JerichoBooks.com

This author is represented by D.C. Jacobson and Associates.

Printed in the United States of America

RRD-C

First Edition: May 2014

10 9 8 7 6 5 4 3 2 1

Jericho Books is an imprint of Hachette Book Group, Inc.
The Jericho Books name and logo are trademarks of Hachette Book Group, Inc.

The Hachette Speakers Bureau provides a wide range of authors for speaking
events. To find out more, go to www.HachetteSpeakersBureau.com or
call (866) 376-6591.

The publisher is not responsible for websites (or their content) that are not
owned by the publisher.

Library of Congress Cataloging-in-Publication Data has been applied for.

For Rosie and Dassi

Contents

Foreword

I first met John when he stepped off a Sea Beaver plane in the Canadian wilderness. Several of us met to plot and scheme about how to love and live better stories.

Hours later, we piled in boats and I dropped John and others off one-by-one at the base of rocky cliffs a hundred miles from the nearest roads, to spend time alone reflecting in quiet solitude.

When I came back to pick John up a few hours later, I found him standing on the top of a tall cliff. But instead of climbing down to get in the boat, he *jumped*. I'm not kidding. He grabbed his knees and did a cannonball.

Since that trip, John and I have become close friends. He attacks life like he climbed that cliff. He relentlessly loves his wife, his daughters and strangers like he's doing a cannonball. He is a fierce and loyal advocate. He is a hero for the fatherless. Best of all, he is my friend. He'll be yours too after you finish reading this book.

The Heroic Path is his learning journey.

It is part poetic, part prophetic. It is raw and gripping. John leads us into the deep end of manhood. Not the shallow "Let's Be Macho" end. Like John, this book is full of soul and life and risk.

It is for the man who realizes we've gone off course and need to find the path again and start walking. At the core of his message is this statement: "The men who change history are those who love well." I think John is right. Love is a force. And John's brand of love is a force of nature.

This book will push you, comfort you, move you, provoke you, and disrupt you. It is witty and insightful, risky and provocative.

I am so glad to introduce you to my friend John Sowers.

—Bob Goff, *New York Times*
bestselling author of *Love Does*

THE
HEROIC
PATH

CHAPTER ONE

The Murdock Files

Manhood feels like a mysterious destination.
This is where we start the journey.

I watched helplessly as Kari struggled for her next breath. The room was chock-full of doctors and nurses, with surgeons on call, waiting for our twins to arrive. Kari had been in labor a full day, but it didn't matter. We had waited nine months and a lifetime.

Now we were ready. Ready to feel those tiny hands squeeze our fingers. Ready to see the color of their eyes. Ready to hear their first cries.

Kari was strong and determined.

She was radiant. Fierce and beautiful like a Nordic queen.

Sahara Rose came out first, squirming like a tadpole. With a head full of raven black hair and compassion on her brow, she was bright and full of spirit and life and soul. We called her Rosie.

Hadassah Ruth came out next, crying and flapping. She was full of music and laughter and sound and joy. The nurses put her on Kari's chest. Her tiny cries sounded exactly like a little bird, "*Laa...Laa...Laa!*" So we called her Little Bird.

From somewhere outside my body, I heard myself yell.

Before that moment, I wasn't sure how I would react. Some men faint or cry. My yell was a mixture of relief and triumph. Until then, I had held every emotion in check: concern, fear, doubt, and excitement. The yell sprang up from some hidden place deep within, booming outward, no longer able to be contained.

After the nurses weighed and cleaned the girls, we held them.

They were wrapped and swaddled tight, like little burritos. I held them as if they were made of flower stems and fine china. In those first moments, everything stopped. We were struck, as if by a force. Two gorgeous baby girls—two immortal souls left their home in the womb and entered the world, drawing their first tender breaths. We didn't say much. We just looked at them and each other, smiling.

I didn't know what I would feel when they were born. I hadn't carried them for nine months. Kari already had this built-in connection, as the girls were conceived, formed, and grew in her womb. This was my first touch.

As I held them, my heart doubled in size.

The nagging and bothering things—the things that tried to make me worried and upset—they just slipped away. Slinked back to the waiting room to sit on the stale, mauve-colored hospital couches. They'd be back, but for now they were gone.

Although the doctors and nurses had seen thousands of births, they paused. They stopped and shared our joy. Life had broken through. It was more powerful than any professional numbness they might be tempted to feel. We were all kissed by the supernatural, witnessing something more beautiful than a thousand sunrises.

Our shared joy combusted into a moment of holy silence.

We all got quiet. It felt really true.

We slowly made our way back to our room. Then, without warning, the nurses handed us the babies and walked off. It was nonchalant, like they were handing me a box of pepperoni pizza—"*Here you go!*" Just like that, the nurses were gone. They didn't tell us what to do, show us how to hold them, or give us a field guide.

I had no idea.

As I watched the girls that first night, I had two distinct emotions.

One: profound joy.

Two: buck-naked fear.

Full disclosure: I'd felt this way for nine months. I had no idea how to be a dad. I never saw one in action. And I still didn't really feel like a man.

My friend Bob clued me in a little. He told me as the father of daughters, I was homeland security. Even though I didn't know what I was doing, I knew how to *protect*. So I stood guard over them like a stone sentry, hovering over their cribs for most of that first night, watching them breathe, their tiny chests rising and falling.

Little Bird coughed once, so I quickly called the nurse. "*Is that normal?*" I pleaded. She gave me two thumbs up, smiled, and left again.

I suddenly became fiercely overprotective of my girls and of Kari—which was good, right? My being overprotective was about fear, but it was instinctive and primal. If anyone messed with my family, I wanted to grow Wolverine's adamantium claws and go into a berserker rage.

I think my fear was more about *inadequacy*.

I was never good at relating, or dating, or talking with girls, so how could I possibly deal with two more? One was hard enough. Now I was seriously outnumbered. Besides, I grew up bow hunting and breaking stuff. Whenever I needed to "find myself," I just went into the woods. In my hood, we shot bottle rockets and roman candles at each other. For fun.

Now I was expected to talk about makeup, dresses, and eventually...boys?

Yeah.

Raising girls didn't feel so instinctive and primal. It felt more like being the only guy trapped in a tea party, with those older women who wear big hats and feather boas. "No...no...*no*..." the tea ladies would correct me in their British accents. "You poor little man, that is terribly, terribly wrong. Hold the teacup like this."

How does a guy possibly fit in there?

Sure, I could fake it. But eventually I'd trip over my feather boa and spill tea on someone's hat. I just don't belong in a tearoom. It reminds me of something Garrison Keillor once said: "It's like a bear riding a bicycle. He can be trained to do it for short periods, but he would rather be in the woods doing what bears do there."[1]

As I stood watching over my girls that first night, fear stalked me like a dark thing. Like Something Awful conjured up from my childhood—a cousin to one of those hairy, long-armed creatures that lived under my bed. Creepers.

Even if I pulled the covers over my head and pretended to be asleep, Something Awful was still there. Waiting. Breathing its hot, rancid breath on the back of my neck.

As a boy, whenever I got out of bed, I never just stepped off. I leaped for dear life, trying to get several feet of distance. The last thing you want is some Creeper grabbing a'holt of your ankle. Then you're toast.

I always knew, one day, they would get me. I felt like one of those helpless girls in a horror movie, trying to get away from a stalker. Mysteriously, she falls down again and again and then totally forgets how to run. The stalker is coming...walking...

slowly. It's twitching and foaming at the mouth. All you can do is crawl on all fours. And sob like a little girl.

I suspect a lot of us guys feel this way.

We all face fear. We all face Something Awful.

Whether a job or a relationship, we all face things that test us. Recession. Job loss. Divorce. Death of a spouse, a parent, or a friend. These things require courage and resilience. When we meet Something Awful, he growls at us and makes us wonder if we can take the next step. He makes us question if we're even men at all.

For me, a surprising thing happened.

When Rosie and Little Bird arrived, I held them and could see in their eyes they needed me. Fear was eclipsed by love and my resolve hardened. Although I didn't have a clue about being a dad, I loved these girls enough to go to hell and back for them. Even though we'd just met, I'd gladly have a bloody knife fight with the devil to protect them.

Love gave me confidence. Determination.

But I still didn't know where to start.

Growing up without a dad, granddad, or uncle around, I felt lost at sea. I didn't have a constant role model for "dad." Manhood seemed out of reach. Like it belonged to a group of elusive guys somewhere over there.

Those guys had big jawlines and were taller than me. They knew how to fix a V8 engine, frame a house, wrestle a gator, then get home in time to shower, shave with a straight razor, put on a suit, and ride the white horse to the ball.

Around those guys, I felt like a poser.

I felt more like Murdock from *The A-Team*.

The A-Team is a group of crack commandos imprisoned for

crimes they didn't commit. Now they're out of prison and are mercenaries for good. They shoot machine guns, fly choppers, blow up stuff, save the girl. Miraculously, no bad guy ever dies. In my mind, the A-Team represents four primal-man archetypes:

1. Hannibal is the confident leader who loves it when the plan comes together. And it does, every time. At the end of every show, Hannibal smiles and lights a big, fat Cuban stogie— of which he has an endless supply.
2. Face is good with the ladies. He's always talking and charming his way into and out of trouble. He's good with words and can handle a machine gun. Face always plays a key role in the master plan.
3. B. A. Baracus (played by Mr. T) is the warrior. He has a huge Mohawk, a perma-scowl, and punches his way through everything. He growls a lot and definitely has anger issues. He calls the bad guys "Sucka!" The only thing that ever gets in his way is Murdock.
4. Murdock is, well, Murdock. Although he can fly a helicopter, he's more an unnecessary appendage. In the middle of a fierce gunfight, Murdock is probably up in a tree making bird noises. Or hiding somewhere, dressed as a woman. Or talking incessantly about nothing, which B.A. calls "jibber jabber." B.A. shouts at Murdock: "Knock off that jibber jabber, Sucka!"

I never felt like Hannibal or Face, as leading other men was foreign. Romancing women seemed like a confusing riddle. I wanted to be hardcore like B.A. but I'm not even strong enough to carry his massive bling.

Most of the time, I just felt like Murdock.

The comic-relief guy. The cop-out. Goofy. Life was much easier as Murdock, because expectations were lower. You didn't have to be charming, strong, or leaderly. You could just be, well…weird.

Manhood still feels weird.

Like one of those oddball cars in Portland. You see them from time to time, painted lime green, covered with bumper stickers, robot toys, prosthetic limbs, action figures, and deer antlers. Even the hood is covered. It's like they had a bunch of garage sale stuff that didn't sell, so they just glued it all over their car.

Manhood feels like I'm spelunking without a flashlight. I'm crawling and bumbling around in the cave, trying to find my way through the bat guano and the blackness and the muck. But I keep bumping into stuff.

Manhood feels hard to hold on to. Slippery.

As a child, I used to break my milk glass nearly every night. True story. I didn't mean to. I just dropped it. Or set it down too hard. Either way, it ended up on the floor in pieces. It got so bad that my mom put my milk in plastic cups and left them on the kitchen counter. Whenever I got thirsty, I had to walk from the living room to the kitchen to get my cup.

I still break stuff.

Add Williams-Sonoma to *The Places I Could Never Work* list.

The man-skills we are expected to have—fixing a leaky faucet, wielding steel, changing the oil, chopping down trees, hooking up the TV, punching a wolf in the face—in these things, I feel woefully inadequate. If manhood is connected to the stereotypical man-skills, I'm a goner. And in our post–industrial revolution world, there are rare few sacred man spaces left.

One is in front of the BBQ grill.

Another is around power tools.

A third is under the hood of a car.

But when *my* car breaks, I go to the mechanic. When he asks what is wrong with my car, I'm lost. No idea. I can't tell the difference between the fan belt and the flux capacitor. So I bluff. The mechanic takes one look at me, and usually has mercy. He acts nice; he acts like he can't tell I'm bluffing. But he knows. He knows.

I'm sure he meets a lot of guys who bluff. And when he finally tells me the car diagnosis, I smile and nod. Just smile and nod. Sometimes it feels like I smile and nod my way through life.

I violate most of the unspoken rules of manhood:

- I ask for driving directions.
- I get lost in Home Depot.
- I need help fixing stuff.

Case in point: I tried to replace our bathtub stopper. I pushed and turned and grunted for about forty-five minutes. Nothing. Nada. Fail. I finally resigned myself to asking my wife for help. With a smile, she instantly popped it into place.

From somewhere deep inside, I heard Mr. T whisper, *Sucka!*

The other day, I had to call my father-in-law to tell me how to start the lawn mower. Our lawn had, over the past several weeks, turned into something akin to a rain forest. But as he explained how to operate the mower, he might as well have been speaking Turkish. Something about thirty-weight engine oil, priming the pump, rolling the starter, and igniting the Bram Stoker.

I didn't get it all.

I tried to start it. I really did.

I primed and pumped and poured gas and pulled the cord. Again and again and again. At the end of two hours, all I had was a gas puddle on the garage floor, and the mower just sat there, staring at me. I swear it was laughing. So I yanked it out of the garage and threw it on the driveway for spite.

It stayed there for two days.

But I've always been a glass-half-full kind of guy. So I decided to ditch the lawn mower idea; I might just be more of a weed-eater man. I had visions of me wearing gnarly, postapocalyptic, *Book of Eli* flight goggles. Some big, crusty, steel-toed boots. Urban camo shorts and fingerless gloves. A wicked machete strapped to my back. I would become *The Avengean*, slinging my machete and flaying weeds into a swift and certain demise.

After a bit of online weed-eater research, I put on my Carhartts and Justin boots, then went to Home Depot. After strutting around, spitting, and acting like an old pro, I picked one of the best weed-eaters I could find, an Echo. It had all the bells and whistles, like an extreme-weed setting, voice activation, and zombie-chopping mode.

Boom.

When I got home, I realized I needed a specific alchemy, an oil-gas mixture, to start it. No biggie. So I went back to Home Depot and bought a gas can, went to the gas station, and got a couple gallons of petrol. Then, I created my sludge fuel, filled the tank, and primed that sucker.

After two hours of busted-knuckle frustration, it finally started. With a devilish grin, I chopped and thrashed weeds for about fourteen seconds.

Then the orange plastic string broke off.

Something Awful wheezed and choked on a laugh.

I'm still not sure why that stuff breaks so easy. Can someone please make some heavy-duty weed-eater string stuff? Okay, I thought, I can do this. So I took off my goggles and, using a screwdriver, took the head off to install more plastic string.

When I did, screws and parts and bolts flew out all over the driveway. A million pieces. So I punted. Put all the pieces in a glass mason jar and waited for my father-in-law to come back into town. I guess we would have weeds a few more weeks.

Yesterday, Kari asked me to assemble and install one of our baby car seats. "Of course," I replied. Undaunted. How hard can that be? I mean, *they are baby seats.* It's not like rebuilding a Hummer.

But after about ten minutes, I realized I needed a Ph.D. in engineering and ten years' hard-labor experience to do it. Or a crack squad of NASA rocket scientists. I worked and pulled and tugged and gritted my teeth.

Nope.

A little later, Kari brought out the other car seat, perfectly assembled and ready for action. Wow, I thought, she's good.

Curious, I asked her, "Well done! How did you do that so fast?"

"I didn't," she replied. "Meredith did."

"Meredith, as in our seventeen-year-old babysitter, Meredith?"

"Yep."

"Seriously?"

"Yes. And I can ask her to do the other one if you want."

"Uh...okay."

My inner Mr. T fell silent. Then he shook his head in disgust and walked away.

I need directions. A compass. A *blueprint.*

Manhood feels like a mysterious destination. Like a remote ManCave with lots of bearded men, and smoke and fire and drum circles. The bearded men don't talk a lot; they just grunt and eat red meat. Somehow, they have man-skills. They aren't trying to prove anything. They're just simply men-in-the-raw. Undomesticated and unfettered. Somehow they are the *initiated*. They drink deep from the draughts of manhood.

For me, this book is about getting to the ManCave.

CHAPTER TWO

Man Guides

Our greatest challenge as men is to carry our
assigned weight.

B ut it's not like Gandalf shows up at my door with a bunch of swarthy dwarves to help me find the way. Even though that would be odd, it would be clear. I would have a guide. A mentor. *Direction.*

Gandalf would have a crusty old map, or a talisman, or something cool to help me find the ManCave. Sure, there might be trolls, massive spiders, werebears, goblins, dragons, and a demented Halfling that wants to eat me.

But at least I would know the way.

In my current state, asking me to find the ManCave is sketchy. It's like someone blindfolded me, spun me around, and told me to pin the tail on the donkey. What I don't know is the donkey lives in Tibet. The joke's on me. I try to pin the tail, I really do. But I wander around aimlessly, then wind up somewhere really random. Like Rancho Cucamonga.

Getting to the ManCave is a flimsy, overgrown path. It's jagged and full of thorns. It runs through haunted woods, tunneling under dark mountains, and through long miles of swamps and endless bogs. I think the biggest reason we don't know the way is because many of us have never seen it.

We have never seen a man walk the path.

Sure, we grew up watching men on-screen. Harrison Ford running from boulders. Denzel Washington prowling across the apocalypse. Dave Grohl singing with vein-popping intensity. Guys, who from the outside, seem to weigh heavy on the man-scale.

But we haven't really *seen* a man. Up close.

We haven't grown up alongside men.

We haven't seen a man plow his fields. Work the steel mills. Use his leathery hands on the plough. We haven't seen the preindustrial-revolution man labor with sweat and bone. We haven't seen a generation fight to save the world. We haven't seen a man fish long days, hunt for dinner, or pray on his knees.

Unlike our forefathers, we are *indoors*.

We live crammed into claustrophobic airplane seats and soulless cubicles. We are tucked away in hipster coffee shops. Or gathered around the plastic-veneered conference room table. We work in climate-controlled air, with moisturized and manicured hands, typing on our MacBooks and iPads.

We have nothing to hunt or gather. No one to fight.

And we haven't grown up in the company of men. We have limited exposure, especially to the men in our own homes—*our fathers.* Jay Z puts words to our story:

> You know my pop left when I was young. He didn't teach me how to be a man, nor how to raise a child, or treat a woman. Right? So of course, my karma, the two things I need I don't have. Right? And I have a daughter. It's the paranoia of not being a great dad.[1]

Amen. How can we be great dads when we're not even sure how to be men? How can we be husbands and fathers when we've never seen one? When Dad is not around, we just make our own conclusions.

My conclusions were that men were a rare, endangered species, like Snuffleupagus. They were like my T-ball coaches, scruffy and oily. They smoked pipes, drove old Jeep Grand Cherokees, and chewed tobacco.

Coach Castle hid behind thick-rimmed glasses, the kind of two-toned jobbies you saw in the seventies. He didn't talk a lot, other than the sparse "good job," or "keep your head down." This made him hard to figure. So I just stared at him, squinting, like he was standing with his back to the afternoon sun.

I was drawn to him. I don't know what it was, he just emitted the secret man-vibe. I felt calmer around him. Protected. I felt temporary acceptance, like I was a visitor to his man-fraternity. And hopefully, someday, I'd be invited to join.

We've seen different guys play the role.

I imagine seeing them at the neighborhood pool.

Gym Guy and *Huge Pickup Truck Guy* are doing cannonballs.

Huge Pickup Truck Guy has a huge 750 T-Rex. It has 50-inch wheels, flames and skulls on the side, and a license plate that says "BIG UN." When he fires it up, it sounds like a pack of growling wolves.

Every morning, he picks up *Gym Guy* and they ride together to work out. *Gym Guy* carries a gallon of water and a backpack full of protein powder. He has barbed wire tattoos, blond tips, and he tans too much, which gives his skin an angry red tint. On the way to the gym, they crank up Nickelback.

At the gym, they grunt and test themselves. Unlike their post–industrial revolution brothers, they work with their hands. They own the macho, tough-guy man vibe. Bravado. This *Bravado Man* is easy to latch on to. He talks loud and has a gaggle of nodding followers.

Something seems amiss. Behind the tattoos and loud trucks seems to be an insecurity, an over-concern about others. *Bravado*

Man wants street cred—and he's determined to prove to everyone else he has it. There's definitely nothing wrong with owning a truck or working out. But we settle for less when our identity is tied to a bench press or a truck.

At the other end of the pool, *Adultlescent Man Guy.*

He is shooting a water gun at the lifeguard. He's trapped in perpetual adolescence. Unemployed but content. He spends long days playing video games. Stuck as a squandering man-boy-child. Unable to step into adulthood, he's a willing victim to his own low expectations. With no vision, his story is small and self-centered.

Playing over in the kiddie pool, we find *MotherBoy.* He wears orange floaties and swims beside Mom. He is safe, well manicured, and he apologizes for everything. His life feels like one big apology. When he sees *Huge Pickup Truck Guy* at the water fountain, he breaks eye contact.

He is like Buster from *Arrested Development.* Buster attends an annual dance with his mom called MotherBoy. The other boys at the dance are preteens. Buster and his mom, Lucille, have attended MotherBoy for twenty years. Lucille rants to Michael, the responsible brother. She says, "Now that your father has deserted us, Buster is impossible to control. Suddenly, he's too much of a big-shot to brush Mother's hair."[2]

MotherBoy lives frustrated. Trapped in the middle of who he is and who Mom wants him to be. He brags about Mom, then lashes out. Defends her, then dates her rival. He joins the Army to spite her, hissing, "Take that, Mother!"

I give these guys a hard time, because I see a lot of them in me.

But I have met a few Man Guides along the way.

Rare men who pointed me to True North. It's hard to say how

I found them—I guess I recognized manhood when I saw it. The man-soul has *weight*, gravity.

My friend Joshua e-mailed me a picture of one of these Guides. His name is Salvatore.

In the picture, Salvatore is receiving the Congressional Medal of Honor, the highest honor our country gives. At the time, he was the only living recipient in the past forty years. Since Vietnam, the award had been granted nine times—all posthumously.

His Army unit was stationed in Northeast Afghanistan, in a place called Korengal Valley. Korengal was a center of terrorist activity, and ground zero for bloodshed. The soldiers called it "The Valley of Death," because in three years, forty-two American soldiers were killed in the Valley. Hundreds of others were wounded.

Around midnight, Salvatore's unit was on patrol, walking single-file down a rocky ridge. After moving 100 yards from base...

Hell exploded.

Terrorists opened fire from *thirty feet away*. Unloaded AK-47 rifles, RPGs, and two heavy machine guns. The fighting was so close the Apache choppers overhead could not return fire, in fear of hitting their own men.

Pause: An RPG is a rocket-propelled grenade, roughly the size of a deflated football, fired from the shoulder. They're used to blow up helicopters, armored cars, and tanks. If one of these rockets hit your friendly neighborhood Prius, it would flip it over backward and turn it into a charred husk. Now, imagine having these things shot at you from the other side of the coffee shop.

The man on point was hit by multiple bullets and knocked flat. Another man was shot in the helmet, and went spinning to the ground. It was a well-planned ambush. They were sitting ducks. Trapped under an avalanche of bullets and rockets, the unit scrambled to find cover. Because of their position, the best they could do was hide behind limited cover and wait for backup.

But Salvatore knew there were fallen men ahead.

So he charged.

He threw grenades and used the explosions for cover. Running blindly in the dark, he wasn't sure of where he was going or where the enemy was.

He had to move. Forward.

He was shot twice. Even though his Kevlar vest was designed to stop a bullet, it still felt like taking a 150 mph fastball in the chest. But he got back up. Threw grenades. Pressed on. Got closer.

Salvatore charged through the wall of gunfire and rockets because his friends were still out there. Finally, he reached the first man. After he checked on the man, another soldier arrived and gave medical care to stop the bleeding.

But there was still another man down. So Salvatore went back into the fray. Bullets were throwing up dirt all around him. It was too dark to aim, so Salvatore shot at enemy muzzle flashes.

He was close. As he crested a small hill, he saw the unthinkable: Two enemies were dragging away one of his friends. Salvatore never stopped.

He rushed forward and shot both enemies, killing one and wounding the other, who fled. He reached his fallen friend, who was badly wounded and bleeding. They were still being fired upon. Somehow Salvatore managed to drag him back to a makeshift cover, and then he worked for an hour to stop his bleeding.

The medevac finally arrived and the Apaches cleared the hills of the enemy. When the battle was over, every man had a bullet hole or shrapnel in his gear. Five were wounded. Two men gave their lives. During the award ceremony, the president gave these remarks:

> Staff Sergeant Salvatore Giunta, repeatedly and without hesitation, you charged forward through extreme enemy fire, embodying the warrior ethos that says, "I will never leave a fallen friend." Your actions disrupted a devastating ambush before it could claim more lives. Your courage prevented the capture of an American soldier. Salvatore risked his life for his fellow soldiers—because they would risk their lives for him. That's what fueled his bravery—not just the urgent impulse to have their backs but the absolute confidence that they had his.[3]

Salvatore risked his life for his friends.

When honored, he deflected the credit. He insisted he was just *doing his job*. He was being a sergeant. Fittingly, "Salvatore" means *savior*.

History is built on the shoulders of men like Salvatore.

Men who stand firm in the face of fear. Charge headlong into the impossible. Rise above evil and terror and limitation. Sacrifice their lives for others. Fight injustice. End slavery. Overthrow dictators. Rescue the oppressed and become a voice for the voiceless. The legacies of these men inspire us, and if we let them, they *invite* us into greatness.

My life feels a million miles away from Korengal Valley. I've never been an Army Ranger. I've never flown an Apache or an A-10 Warthog. When I hear about Salvatore, something dormant comes alive in me.

Something *awakens*.

This also happens when I watch movies about those who sacrifice for the greater good. I get motivated, have a brief awakening, then settle back down into numb domestication. I hear the comforting voices of the tea ladies. They pat me on the head and say, "Come sit back down, honey. Calm down. Have a cookie."

I like the tea ladies. They smell like dehydrated rose petals. They make good biscotti. They watch soap operas, and they have shelves of old, dusty books without jackets. They are gentle souls and never kick me out of their club.

But when I overstay my welcome, my vision gets blurry, like one of those long-exposure pictures of the highway. You can see the red and the white lights of cars streaming by, but nothing is in focus. The call of the wild grows faint.

Whenever I leave the tearoom and head back to the woods, I find clarity.

I remember standing ankle deep in the living movement of the White River. It was the dawn of my twentieth birthday, eleven days before Midsummer's Eve, but still the spring of my journey.

I walked downstream. A few hundred yards from my tent, I surprised a white-tailed buck. He still had his summer velvet on his antlers. After he left, only the cliffs and the crisp mountain air remained.

Standing in those clear waters, I closed my eyes and reflected on my first twenty years of life. And how I wanted to live the next twenty. I thought about what kind of man I was becoming—and dreamed about the man I wanted to be at forty.

In that water, I knew I could do anything. These moments fuel possibility and awaken imagination. Awaken me to the wildness of the masculine soul. These moments call me to something more.

How do we step out of the tea party and onto the treacherous path? How do we transcend the mundane, the routine, and the ordinary? What separates the millions clamoring for greatness from the one like Salvatore?

Honestly, I don't know. But his story tells me:

Men stand tallest when they stand for others.

I felt this when I became a dad. I had stood for others before—family or friends or teammates. When my girls were born, the protector voice was louder than the voice of fear. It surprised me. It felt right, deeply right. I liked being a protector.

You can see the protector even in young boys.

I heard about a seven-year-old boy who shielded his younger brother and friend from a rabid dog. He grabbed the two boys—who were four years old—and threw them under a car while he fought off the dog. He fought for a long time, until a man finally came to their rescue with a shovel.

The great stories are other-centered.

They fly in the face of self-absorption. They stand in opposition to the enticing lures of self-love. Cowardice is, after all, heightened self-interest. Soldiers don't flee with the intention of hurting others. In fact, they're not thinking of others at all. They're just trying to save themselves.

God hardwired men to live and die for others.

As Salvatore said, this is our job. Our responsibility. Salvatore's story is a bold contrast against the millions of dads who bail. A man is like my cousin, NoRemo, a Marine who quietly and faithfully served two tours in Iraq. A man is *Semper Fi*—always faithful.

But our Great Temptation is to *escape*.

We want to shirk our responsibilities. Men are ditching jobs. Families. We are tempted to have a midlife crisis, to move to a secluded beach, date another woman, and forget everything and everyone for whom we are responsible.

This is part of the Curse. The thorns and thistles of our work and life get painful and tiring and old. We just want to get away.

But men are like pickup trucks—we do best when we have weight in the truck bed. On icy roads, we tend to skid around when there is no weight over the rear tires. We perform best when we carry a load, when others count on us. This is when we rise, when we find our strength.

Our greatest challenge as men is to carry our assigned weight.

Carrying our weight means doing the things only we can do, the things which we are responsible. Our thoughts, our actions, and our words. One of our most crucial responsibilities is our relationship with our family. With the Almighty. Being faithful in the small things at work. Being a brother and a loyal friend. Serving the greater community. The specifics look different for each one of us. We may not know how to carry our weight, but love calls us to figure it out.

We are all tempted to despair, to get discouraged and stall out. Or we're tempted to avoid the weight by getting lost in leisure, in games and sports and chasing does. We pursue pleasure and are free rangers, but all the while, our unused work tools are left in the shed—dull and rusty.

This man has no vision for stewarding his gifts—or making the most out of his time. He coasts along, living for his own self-amusement. George MacDonald tells this man, "You can't live on amusement. It's the froth on the water—an inch deep, and then the mud."

Since the first man, Adam, we have struggled with fidelity. We want to dump the weight. And many do. Men are wilting, leaving. Bailing out on life, spouses, and families. The evening news is littered with the wreckage. Other men never bail, but never fully engage either. They never pick up the weight.

They just go limp, passive.

They isolate themselves. Get lost in Sports Center. In the *Walking Dead* zombie apocalypse, or under the armchair numbers of Fantasy Football. We dream about the life we wish we had. So we dump our weight for others to carry.

Some men numb out, overeat, oversleep, avoid. We live in a hazy, alcoholic fog—wasting away on cheap beer, while the world goes madly on. No one can carry our weight for us. It is ours alone to carry. Our legacy is made or marred by how we carry it.

Millions quit. Others stand firm under the weight. And when we do, we find our strength. I think being a man is making the stubborn, daily choice to carry our own weight, even when all hell breaks loose around us.

CHAPTER THREE

The Road Goes Ever On

We are a generation of men without place. When
we find place, we find our strength.

For me, carrying the weight means figuring out how to be the best man I can be. Figuring out how to be a husband and a dad, learning how to be faithful with the gifts and time I've been given. Even when Something Awful is staring and drooling at me.

This is especially true, when I feel overwhelmed or under-equipped. When it feels like I'm camping on Mount Hood without the right gear. It's raining, my tent is leaking, and my sleeping bag is a soggy mess.

Love fuels our courage.

Courage tells us to keep going. Love-born courage takes different forms. It can be obvious and public—like taking a bullet for someone. Or rushing into burning buildings one morning in September.

Courage can come as a whisper—a quiet act of selflessness. Forgiving a friend. Giving blood or an anonymous gift. Writing that letter to your dad, the one you should have written a long time ago.

Sometimes courage is just moving in the right direction. Mary Anne Radmacher wrote, "Courage doesn't always roar. Sometimes courage is the quiet voice at the end of the day saying, 'I will try again tomorrow.'"[1]

When my girls were born, they were healthy but under-weight, like most twins. Everything about them was *tiny*—tiny little cries. Tiny little hands. Tiny crooked smiles. Their tiny mouths were too small to nurse. We fed them with syringes. We put our pinky fingers in their mouth, and gave them syringes of expressed milk.

We did this every two hours, for a couple of months. Feeding our babies with a syringe wasn't in the books. Speaking of books, there are 1,974,131,892 parenting books. We read them all. Books like:

- *Breast Pumps—Bouncy Seats—and Tummy Time!*
- *Potty-Train Your Baby in Forty-Two Minutes!*
- *Real Men Wear Baby-Bjorn!*
- *Swaddle It, Swaddle It!*

None of them said anything about syringes. Kari jumped right in like a pro, nursing and feeding. But I still felt like the kid who broke his milk glass. Every two hours, my job description looked like this:

Stagger out of bed around 11:00 p.m.

Step on a baby toy.

Try not to scream bloody murder.

Hop on one foot over to the refrigerator and prepare a syringe.

Spill breast milk everywhere.

Trip over the crib to pick up a crying baby in the dark.

Try not to wake up the other baby.

Inject milk with laser-guided precision and perfect tempo.

Do it again for the other baby in forty-five minutes.

At first, it was alarming. Uh, no, not alarming. Bewildering. It was like water-skiing, without skis. Water dragging. That's pretty much how I water-ski.

The one time I tried to ski, I wound up drinking the lake. I was clinging to the rope with one hand, getting ricocheted through bouncy waves like a tetherball. All I could do was shout through the waves, gagging on water, "Go, go, go... just keep going!"

I think my girls were as shocked-and-awed as I was.

I'm sure being out in the open air, outside of their watery womb-home, breathing oxygen for the first time, drinking milk from a syringe—all felt surreal. The girls were trying to figure out how to be babies. How to eat for the first time, communicate, and what to do with new emotions: hunger, fear, fatigue.

While they were learning how to be babies, I was learning how to be a dad. It felt like someone had blindfolded me, tied me up, and then stuffed me into the pouch of a giant kangaroo named "Skippy."

None of us knew what we were doing.

Rosie cried nearly every night with an upset tummy. She woke up in pain. Afraid. The worst part of it was her terrified expression. Her crying was awful to hear. It put your nerves on edge. Crying babies—especially when they are yours—put your brain on high alert. Crying babies on a four-hour airplane ride can be an irritation.

But when they're *your* babies, it's different.

You love your babies, which is why the crying kills you.

I'm sure there are a bunch of scientific studies on this by Harvard, Cornell, and other smart colleges that say a baby crying turns your nerves into spaghetti. The experts say it's like having ten thousand screaming birds of prey descend on your head and perch on your cochlear nerve. They say a baby crying is powerful enough to wake up a hibernating yeti.

Whatever. They're the experts. I just know it gets my

adrenaline flowing. The crying makes me feel helpless and inadequate. It makes me feel like I'm letting them down. Especially when they get old enough to say something that resembles "Pa-pa." They cry and say, "Pa-pa, pa-pa, pa-pa," over and over again. Then it really gets you.

In those 1:00 a.m. moments, you come nose-to-nose with Something Awful. He looks like a bully—mocking you and telling you that you're worthless. He asks, "Hey, aren't you that guy that always needs your wife to help? The guy who needs his seventeen-year-old babysitter to fix his stuff?"

He sits there on your couch, stinking and wheezing. He gloats at you with a snorty little laugh. The longer he sits there, the bigger and more brazen he gets. He tells me I am inadequate, and then waits for me to me fail, like a giant trap-door spider.

Here it was: 1:00 a.m.

Rosie desperate and depending on me to do something.

Anything. I had no idea what.

But when you love someone, *you figure it out*.

I figured out how to quiet her by laying her across my arm, placing her tummy on the warmth of my arm and chest, like a heating pad. It worked. Somehow. I gained confidence. My courage grew. A little.

This became our nightly routine: Rosie falling asleep on my arm at 1:00 a.m.

After I put Rosie down, it was Little Bird's turn.

She didn't have an upset tummy but she cried and sang all the same. So I picked her up, kissed her tiny curls and her tiny ears, then gave her some milk. She cuddled in, chewed on her sleepy sack, and went back down.

Even though we were new at this, we were in it together. We

were learning together, on the fly. Those early victories gave me nudges of encouragement.

—You can do this—

I was making it up along the way. Somehow, it was working. Fear was losing its grip. Courage begot courage. I had a long way to go, but we were making progress. Together. It was a massive step.

I was learning the rhythm of "Dad."

But I still had man questions.

These questions made me feel inadequate; they made me afraid to fail. Even though I experienced small wins, I knew Something Awful was just biding his time. He was still out there, lurking. Like Cato from the old Pink Panther movies, he was hiding in the food pantry or in the backseat of my car, waiting for the right moment to pounce. I wasn't sure who would win our next skirmish.

This kind of fear drives many men to quit.

We disengage from life, simply because we are afraid to fail. Men leave jobs, families, and responsibilities. Or we live hidden away from life, in basements or bars, drinking our lives away. Over time, we become wraiths, shadow-men living apart from reality and destiny.

I recently heard a story about a man named Constantine.

He adopted troubled boys from Brooklyn and became "Dad" to them. He invited these boys into his home, taught them self-discipline and how to confront fear. He showed them how to box and how to become men. He gave them family.

He gave them *place*.

Constantine went to the courts to fight for the rights of a thirteen-year-old boy. The boy had dozens of arrests and was already considered a hardened criminal by the state of New York. He made a habit of breaking into cars and convenience stores and getting into fights. He often slept in abandoned buildings, and was described by the judge as a feral child. As Constantine left the courtroom, the judge mocked him: "Good luck with this one."

The boy's dad left shortly after he was born, and the financial load crushed his newly single mom. They were forced to move to the Brownsville section of Brooklyn, and his world was flipped on its chin. He later described Brownsville as "horrific, tough, a gruesome kind of place. Kill or be killed."[2]

His life in elementary school included being bullied and terrorized. In the third grade, someone put a gun in his face. He was robbed—for the few nickels and quarters in his pockets. He ran away. He lived in fear and was ashamed because of it.

The boy liked pigeons. So he stole some money and bought some.

He kept them, trained them, cared for them. Pigeons were his solace. His escape. Until one day, when a fifteen-year-old gang leader found his pigeons and killed one with his bare hands. The boy had seen enough. Even though he was only nine, he beat the older gang leader to an inch of his life.

After the fight, he became the most feared gangster in Brooklyn.

When you grow up with fear, with your back against the wall—you feel trapped. You're one of the weak ones. Trembling. You duck your head, avoid eye contact. You hope they don't smell your fear, which is like blood in the water. You pray to God they don't notice. Because if they do notice, they'll swarm you like a pack of hammerheads. So you hide or you bluff by acting tough.

You learn to look out for yourself. Eventually, you may learn to hit back. Hurt back.

This is what our Brooklyn boy did.

He grew violent and his mother told the court she couldn't control him.

So when he was twelve, he landed in juvenile detention, at the Tryon School for Boys. He was still feral, out of control. He spent his days locked away in solitary confinement. After one fighting incident, the boy requested to meet Bobby Stewart.

Stewart, a fiery Irishman and a former professional boxer, came to Tryon to teach boxing for self-discipline. When he met the boy, Bobby said:

"I understand you want to see me. Let me tell you one thing before you open your mouth. If I get any backtalk or lip from you, I am gone for good. You only get one chance with me, so make it count."

The boy replied, "I want to be a boxer."

Stewart countered, "Every bum in this hole figures themselves a fighter. I haven't found one yet. If you can keep out of trouble for one month, I'll come back and we'll talk again."

Stewart did come back. The two trained together.

The boy was already a man-child. At thirteen, he weighed 200 pounds, and he punched with more ferocity than anyone he had ever seen. Stewart showed him the basics: how to stand, throw a punch, leverage body weight, bob and weave, and slip punches.

Although Stewart was a trained professional, he realized he would soon be no match for the boy. With the proper training, the boy would rule the boxing world.

So he introduced him to Constantine "Cus" D'Amato. Cus

was part monk, part street-tough Italian, part philosopher, and part priest.

Full tactical boxing genius.

Cus embodied the warrior spirit. He trained champions Floyd Patterson and José Torres. Before the famous "Rumble in the Jungle" fight, Mohammed Ali asked Cus how to beat George Foreman. Cus told him. Ali listened. And won.

Cus met the boy when he was fourteen, sparring Stewart. After only two rounds of watching this boy fight, Cus said, "That's the heavyweight champion of the world. If he wants it, it's his." So he invited the boy into his home. Taught him respect. Earned his trust, and trained him as a fighter. A typical training day might look like this:

Wake up at 4 a.m.

Run three miles.

Go back to sleep until 10 a.m.

Bag work on a 300-pound bag (only Rocky Marciano used a 300-pound bag).

Spar.

Lunch—rest.

Lift weights.

Watch film of the great ones.

Over the next few years, Cus molded the boy into the man who became the most destructive force in boxing history.

Iron Mike Tyson.

At twenty, Tyson became the youngest heavyweight champion ever. Using Cus's unique numbering system, superhuman conditioning, and his exclusive "peekaboo" boxing style, Tyson spent the next few years dominating the division like the great ones before him.

Ali. Louis. Marciano. Dempsey.

Tyson hit people so hard it's a miracle no one died.

What people didn't see was the way Cus loved Mike. And his love was giving Mike place. It was giving him confidence and strength. Self-discipline and mastery.

When Cus brought Mike into his home, he *fathered* him.

At first, Mike trusted no one. He was afraid and full of anger. Mike thought Cus was a "crazy old man." But over time, he began to trust and respect Cus. Cus believed in him as a person and a boxer. Mike's fear and anger began to dissipate. In a rare piece of video footage, Cus is sitting beside a teenage Mike, talking about how much he cares for him. In his crusty, Italian accent Cus says:

> I have a very deep affection for him. I do. To me, he's my boy—he's with me. If he weren't here, I probably wouldn't be alive today. He gives me the motivation and interest to stay alive. 'Cause I believe a person dies when they no longer want to live. But I have a reason with Mike here.[3]

In the video, Mike is grinning like a little boy who was just handed a Popsicle. It is a picture of a fatherless boy who never had Dad brag on him. Or be proud of him. Mike is being visibly transformed by the simple, stubborn love of Cus D'Amato.

I know, I know—you are reading this and you're suspicious. All this talk about love and place feels *soft*. It doesn't feel like it could whoop up on a 300-pound heavy bag. Or take down Leon Spinks in 91 seconds. Talking about love and place feels more like a group hug. But this is exactly what happened to Mike.

Love was driving out fear, and Mike was becoming a son.

But right before Mike became champion, Cus passed away. When he died, Mike lost his father, his everything. He later said:

It was like a father-son relationship. When Cus died, I lost my whole life. I didn't know where to go. I can remember his funeral. I was a pallbearer. I was very proud to be a pallbearer. I was just 19 years old. I didn't know what to do with my life. I remember thinking; I don't have my friend no more. I was very scared, I felt lonely. I felt naked to the world. I felt like a very vulnerable young boy.[4]

Mike fought well for a couple of years, but eventually derailed. He lost his focus and self-discipline. He returned to his old gangster ways: drinking and drugs and street fighting. He lost his trainer, Kevin Rooney, who was Cus's handpicked successor. He lost his intense training regimen and he stumbled in the ring, losing to Buster Douglas. Arrested multiple times, he was convicted of rape and thrown in prison.

In a recent interview with Oprah, Mike broke down when talking about Cus. A few months later, Tyson breaks down again when he's inducted into the Boxing Hall of Fame. His love for Cus—thirty years after his death—is so tangible and powerful that Mike cannot talk about it without tears.

Mike was fighting for Cus. After he died, he lost his will to fight. Many critics agree: Mike Tyson could have been the most dominant heavyweight champion in boxing history. But in the end, he beat himself—which was the real tragedy. Years before his fall, Cus said prophetically, "To see a man beaten not by a better opponent, but by himself, is a tragedy."[5]

Many lose their will to fight.

We live in resignation and accept a lesser destiny. This is our real tragedy. When we give up and beat ourselves. It happens when we get lonely, worn-out, or desperate. Or when we forget who we are. Or when we lose our sense of place.

Life did not turn out how we imagined, so we lower our hopes. Once upon a time, our heart was wild and young. Now it feels old and tired. We don't want to fail again, and this fear makes us live defensively. When our hope leaves and heads south for the winter, our life grows dull. We may embrace the sadness and grow depressed. Life becomes less about celebrating, and more about tolerating.

The fire in the belly dies.

From a distance, we admire the fearless man. We admire the man who still lives with the fire, who charges headfirst into life. We long to be like Bruce Wayne out of the pit, get back to Gotham and face Bane. Deep down, we know we're *not* Batman. And we don't know why.

Most of us think we work for strength by doing P90X, getting a barbed wire tattoo, buying all the right gear, eating lots of protein bars and raw eggs, hanging out with *Gym Guy*. Strength belongs to the guys in the ring or on the gridiron, the warriors and the bravado men.

Bravado is surface enthusiasm, not attached to an inner move. It doesn't root a man against fear. When Something Awful shows up, the *Bravado Man* finds the nearest corner and goes to a happy place. Something more is needed than muscle and chanting and acting like *Gym Guy*.

We live in fear because we don't know Cus. We have no fathers, elders, or mentors to show us how to live. Throw a punch.

Be honest. Work through fatigue. Love our families. This is why so many of us struggle with our sexuality, aggression, commitment, strength, responsibility, and our vision as men.

We are a generation of men without place.

We haven't grown up in the company of fathers or other men. We have no man-instruction, lessons, or schooling. We have no models or heroes. We're trying to figure out manhood. We're trying to find place. We don't know the basic stuff or have confidence in our man-skills. We live in fear and inadequacy.

Lao Tzu offers, "Being deeply loved by someone gives you strength, while loving someone deeply gives you courage."[6]

Love gives us strength and place. Love begets place. In turn, place gives us: roots, confidence, identity, and metal. Place is our steel backbone, the adamantium skeleton of our strength.

Man Secret: Place and strength are linked at the hip.

Our strength is hijacked when we don't have place. Naturally, most of us fear failure. Dropping the winning pass. Not having what it takes at our job, or with a woman. The more we listen to the fear, the more it owns us. It grows dark tentacles around us, taking root. Wrapping around our souls, it shows us what will happen when we inevitably fail. It shows us the moment when we are facedown on the mat. What we don't understand, deep in our souls:

Sometimes men *want* to fail.

It's our preemptive strike on fear, if we don't try before we get to the finish line—we never have to face it. If we never show our writing to the publisher, our new idea to our peers, or our dream to the public, we never have to face their rejection.

To relieve ourselves of the fear, we *prefail*.

Failure is inevitable, so we choose it before it happens. We try to put an end to our fear, to our suffering. If we throw in the towel before we fail—we don't have to live under fear anymore. So we fail by sabotaging ourselves. Or with passivity, by never applying ourselves. We never step into the ring. We never roar.

One time, my friend Bob thought it'd be a good idea for me to drive his front-end loader with no lessons or instructions. A front-end loader basically looks like a bulldozer with a tall crane on the front instead of a sled. It was big and green.

Bob just smiled and laughed and said, "*Hey, man! Drive this!*"

He wanted me to use his crane to pick up and move some heavy logs. Tall order. I had lower expectations—my goal was not to drive it off the cliff.

I hopped in the seat and started pushing and pulling levers. Lurching and jerking forward. Then backward. Herky jerky.

Finally, I figured out which levers moved the crane, so I tried to pick up the logs. But I ended up slamming the big arm down onto the ground. Again and again and again. I was hitting the ground so hard that the machine was catching air. No joke.

After five minutes, I accidentally hit one of those accursed logs. But picking one up proved to be a pipe dream. The best I could do was tear off some bark. If those logs had been hungry zombies, they would have eaten me. Or died laughing.

Eventually, Bob put me out of my misery.

I stumbled out, defeated.

Then Bob asked this dainty city girl named Jenny to drive, and I thought, "This is gonna be good. No *way* she will drive this." I looked on with my arms crossed, smirking. I knew my crushed ego would soon be propped up, vindicated by her failure.

Even though it was her first time, Jenny manhandled that front-end loader. She working it perfectly, lifting and lowering logs like some old leathery lumberjack.

Figures. I got owned by a little city girl named Jenny. Ouch.

Add John Deere to my *Places I Could Never Work* list.

Being a man without place feels like sitting behind the wheel of a powerful machine. A machine that can do some pretty awesome stuff. Lift logs. Throw rocks. Woo women. Crush zombies. But once we get in the driver's seat, it's confusing. There are tons of levers, pedals, wheels, gears, retina scans, nitrous oxide, and self-eject buttons. We barely manage to get the thing started, but everything else after that is sketchy.

CHAPTER FOUR

Woman as Salvation

She is a beautiful and mystical creature made in the Garden. But she is not made to carry us.

I found place in the world of women. I learned feminine rhythms, and was more at home in their company. When men find place in the world of women, we are familiar with things like the nesting instinct and seasonal décor. We learn how to share feelings, how to be maternal and receptive.

Here are some random words I learned after I got married:

- Lamaze
- Ramekins
- Duvet covers
- Indirect lighting
- Downward-facing dog

Feminine words, feminine rhythms.

Please understand: I'm not condescending. Nor am I implying women are fragile or materialistic. Women are not overly emotional, or helpless weak creatures. They are not lessor beings or some other ignorant stereotype. These stereotypes anger me.

Listen: My mom is whip-smart and tougher than D2 tool steel. She graduated from *college* at eighteen and works harder than most men. And she can make a snarky car salesman cry. I saw it happen.

Mom worked three jobs to make ends meet.

She still managed to come to my karate tournaments and high school and college baseball games, even when they were out of state. Mom sent us to good schools, got us braces, paid for our sports gear and uniforms, and bought shoes that fit. She kept food on the table and worked her fingers to the bone for us.

For us.

Mom held up the sky for me.

My grandmother moved from the country into the city to help raise us while Mom worked. She picked me up from school every day, arriving an hour early to be first in line. Her old blue Mercury always sat in front of a long line of fancy SUVs and Beamers driven by soccer moms.

When I got in the car, she handed me a homemade Gatorade slushy, in a glass mayonnaise jar carefully wrapped in aluminum foil. It was frozen just right—icy but drinkable. She handed me the slushy and said something nice and grandmotherly, like, "You are such a right handsome young man. I love the way you walk tall, you don't sloop like some of the other boys. You make me so proud."

She was always proud of me.

She drove me home and stayed until Mom returned from work. Mom came back at six or seven, and then worked some more, typing away, doing some legal brief or research or something.

Grandmother got me snacks and sometimes dinner, usually chicken tenders. She watched me run around outside, building forts, throwing pinecone grenades and doing what boys generally do. Sometimes she took me to movies—we saw *The Empire Strikes Back* and *Return of the Jedi* together. These were iconic moments—moments often shared between sons and fathers. Moments that shape us. My grandmother filled those moments.

My grandmother taught me things…how to draw straight lines.

Write cursive.

Love books.

In the summer, she took me to art classes and the library. We did the summer reading program together. I got lost under piles of old, dusty books. I staggered out of the library, satisfied, arms full of books. Like I was carrying Easter eggs or a bag full of Halloween candy.

The library is still my favorite place. It reminds me of her.

On Sundays she took me to All Souls Church. We attended Ladies Aid, the AARP version of Sunday school. Think: Hair spray. Oil of Olay smells. Huge leather Bibles.

The ladies always told me how tall I was, which was weird, because they all seemed like giants to me. I had navy blue shoes called "Kangaroos," which had zipper pouches on the sides, and the ladies gave me nickels for my pouches. Sometimes I got a butterscotch.

Grandmother showed me how to open doors for the ladies at church. I helped them get to their cars. They held on to my arm as they stepped off the curb. Even though I was young, I liked taking care of them. Protecting them. It felt right.

When I left for college, Grandmother sent me a handwritten card every week. She always wrote on a Monet print, filling the card with life. Saying she loved me and was proud of me and was praying for me. She sent her cards, through college and graduate school, once a week for seven years. It didn't matter how many miles I was from home, her love *rooted* me.

I still remember her phone number. The gentle way she carried herself, with humble class. She wore blue Isotoners when she drove—both hands on the wheel. A plaid long-coat she got from Scotland. She got her hair done on Fridays. I remember her sing-songy voice. When she came in the house, she always chirped, "*Woo-hoo!*" to make sure I knew she was there. Sometimes I chirped "*Woo-hoo!*" back.

She believed in me and prayed for me. Never corrected me much, just frowned and said, "*Oh honey, don't do that.*" It worked. She gave her life for us and loved me with quiet, stubborn consistency.

Her love made me who I am. Her love gave me home.

Gave me *place*.

My mom also knew how to be fierce.

She knew I loved the Boston Red Sox, so sometimes we went to Arlington, Texas, to watch them play the Rangers. We always stayed in the team hotel. I sat in the lobby for hours waiting to see the players walk from the hotel over to the ballpark. I met a ton of players. Those trips were highlights of my life.

Some of the players were really cool, like Mike Greenwell and Ellis Burks. Ellis let me carry his bats for him, which, for a twelve-year-old baseball-loving kid, was a dream. It was the night before he flew to Chicago for the All-Star Game. Ellis told me to go get a bunch of stuff for him to autograph. He autographed a hat, a baseball, and baseball cards for me. The next year, he remembered me when I came back to Arlington. Cool dude.

Another time I saw Roger Clemens leaving the team hotel to play golf. Starting pitchers sometimes played golf in the mornings on an off day. Roger is one of the best pitchers in baseball history, and holds the single-game strikeout record, twenty. He won seven Cy Young Awards, went to the All-Star Game eleven times, and won two World Series.

Roger had a mean streak. He wasn't afraid to throw at hitters, "cutting them down at the knees" in his words. Getting hit by a 95 mph fastball in the kidney is not a barrel of laughs. A ton of players said they wanted a piece of him, even his own teammates. But no one ever charged the mound. No one had the guts.

One time, Clemens was pitching in the World Series when Mike Piazza fouled off a pitch and broke his bat. The bat flew right at Clemens, who grabbed it *and threw it back at Piazza*. Now, you need to know the unwritten rules about baseball fights:

1. It is not really a fight; it's a scrum.
2. If the other team charges, your team charges.
3. If someone beans your guy, your pitcher beans him back.

Baseball fights are pushing and shoving, sometimes there is a fist thrown, but not usually. Baseball fights are nothing like hockey fights, with pulling shirts and biting and bloody fists and losing teeth. Those dudes *really* fight.

The goal of the baseball fight is not to beat someone up, but to just run out there, push, and jump around a lot. It's kinda like, *"Hey, guys! We saw what you did, and we're ticked! I mean, really ticked! That's why we are all out here jumping around!"*

I've been in a couple of these fights, and once you get past the red-faced shouting, they're fun. Baseball fights are more like a mosh pit; everyone is pushing and cussing and falling down. It feels like you could probably hire a DJ, turn on the strobe light, and charge admission.

No one in baseball ever throws or hits someone with a bat. No one. Swinging or throwing a bat at someone is not even a consideration.

So in the World Series, when Clemens caught and threw the bat back at Piazza, everyone was stunned. Piazza had a puzzled look on his face, like, *"Dude, what in tarnation was that?"* Benches cleared and there was lots of yammering and jawing—the usual baseball moshing stuff. Nothing substantive. Even the umps were spooked; they didn't kick Clemens out of the game.

So when I saw Roger Clemens in the team hotel in Arlington, it was no small task to ask for an autograph. I felt like I was jumping into a shark tank. Once I started, there was no going back. I walked up to him, and with all the bravery I could muster, I stuttered, "Mr. Clemens, would you please sign my baseball?"

"No way, kid," he snapped. "I've already signed for you."

Crushed.

I couldn't ask him again. So I hung my head, made my slow retreat back into the hotel lobby, crawled under the rug, and lay there like a dead thing. I never felt further from the ManCave.

A few minutes later, Mom came down and could tell I was distraught.

"What's wrong?" she asked.

"Well, Roger Clemens is right there, and when I asked for an autograph, he griped and told me he already signed my baseball."

Mom grabbed the baseball out of my hand and walked outside, where Clemens was about to get into a limo. I could hear her voice from inside the lobby.

"Mr. Clemens!"

He turned around, towering over her a full foot, 230 pounds of lean, mean Texan. She was unflappable.

"Roger, you said you already signed for my son and you didn't. I would be grateful if you would sign this baseball."

You should have seen his body language, he was *backing up,* trying to get away from her. Here was the scariest and mean-est pitcher in baseball history, the guy who threw a bat at the muscle-bound Mike Piazza, and he was *retreating*. He was recoiling from a small Southern woman named Georgia.

I still have that autograph.

We've been raised by heroic moms and grandmoms.

Women who have given everything for us. They who stick up for us, fight for us, wear two hats, work multiple jobs and some-times more. They often do this at great personal cost to themselves, sometimes sacrificing future relationships or opportunities.

Mom is loyal unto death.

When our lives are in chaotic ruin, Mom still loves us. And the most hardened men still love Mom. You see this in prisons all over the world. Fatherless men who are imprisoned for rejecting the authority and laws of "The Man," but still hold allegiance to one person, Mom. Every year, prisoners write millions of Mother's Day cards to prove it.

This is also the pro-athlete narrative. It goes something like this:

Boy is born.

Dad leaves, they never meet.

Single teenage mom raises boy by herself.

She can't pay mortgage, house gets condemned and bulldozed.

She is broke, forcing boy and mom to move twelve times in three years.

Boy starts playing sports—basketball and football. He is good at them.

At eighteen, he graces the cover of *Sports Illustrated* and is named "The Chosen One."

He graduates high school and Nike gives him a $90 million contract at the age of eighteen, *before* he is drafted No. 1 by the NBA's Cleveland Cavaliers.

Then, LeBron buys his mom a mansion and anything else she can imagine. He gives her a "shout-out" from the White House and talks about her in his autobiography.

An NBA commercial called "Family Is Big" features Kevin Durant's mom, Wanda Pratt. (For the uninitiated, the aforementioned LeBron and Kevin Durant are the best two basketball players in the NBA.) This commercial shows Wanda cheering for her son from the sidelines. You can hear Kevin's voice say, "It's all surreal to me. It's a blessing to look around and see all this, and to be honest, I didn't think I would be here. The only one who really believed in me…from day one, was my mom."

For a generation of fatherless boys (and men), Mom is the center.

Mom believes in us until the end. She cheers from the sidelines. She fights to keep a roof over our head. She works three jobs to give us food, clothes, and love.

I remember growing up afraid that, if my mom left, my world would implode and collapse inward upon itself. Years later, I told this to a friend, saying I grew up feeling "stranded on a remote island, and Mom was my guide. If she died, I would fall into a dark pit and never return."

As boys, we might have felt lost and tossed about at sea, but Mom was there—always there—throwing us her rope. She was our lifeline. We white-knuckled that rope with every ounce of strength, made it out of the waves and safely into her boat. But once we finally got to shore, we didn't let go of the rope; we tied it around our waists. Our moms, as caretakers, were happy to let us.

Many men are still tied to Mom.

As long as we are tied to Mom, we're drawing from her feminine energy, learning how to listen and feel and respond and be sensitive. Some of this energy may serve us well in later relationships. But inwardly, we're out of sync.

There is a bristling creature within us, lying dormant. It is wolfish, uncontainable, lying just beneath the surface of our polite veneer. We don't know exactly what it is. But we know if it gets out, it will never go back into the cage. Whatever it is, it is more powerful, ferocious, and terrifying than Something Awful.

So we repress it.

Stay careful and cautious, like Mom says. Avoid conflict. Play on the safe grass. We do exactly as we're told. But we live in tension, in growing frustration—something inside us wants out. It wants to be unleashed; we keep building the fence higher. We avoid the inner conflict and grind our teeth, or sweat through our sheets. We live with displaced anger and confusion.

We are not who we were born to be.

Inside, we feel soft. Passive. We live under Mom's control instead of our wildness.

In my life, this passivity shows up as *indecision*. It rears its head at major life intersections and decisions. I default to passivity when the weight feels heavy. Places where the stakes are raised, like buying a car or a house, or doing anything that requires risk. In these places, I stall. Paralyzed by uncertainty and fear, I fly loopy buzzard circles around the decision. I choose by making no choice, in the name of caution.

I'm careful not to offend. This makes me overly apologetic.

People tell me to stop apologizing so much. When I was a teenager, girls looked at me and told me I would make a great husband and dad someday, but they didn't want to date me. I'm sure they thought I was sweet, "like a little puppy," and giggled after I walked away. I felt like *MotherBoy*.

Men don't sit around kitchens with sweaters tied around their necks, extolling the virtues of living with Mom. But for me, *MotherBoy* came naturally. Mom raised me, and taught me how to relate, ride a bike, and catch a baseball. So, of course, I wanted to please her.

I was never full-blown *MotherBoy*, but I did look to her for everything. It made me more receptive, less decisive. I fell into the pattern of looking to Mom and the world of women for life direction. My life wholly depended on a woman—Mom, so naturally, I looked to other women to fulfill the same role.

We may have offered ourselves to God, but Mom is our salvation.

Mom is our True North. Even though she might look different now. She might be a girlfriend. Or a long line of girlfriends, or a string of one-night stands.

Our misguided reach for Mom takes many forms.

Some look for feminine nourishment in an *image*—a naked, captivating, and mysterious thing. This thing woos us and tells us we're strong and passionate lovers. Promising to heal our wounds, it offers acceptance when we feel alone. It tells us we are sexually desirable; we are competent and capable lovers.

Nothing in creation is as alluring as the feminine body. No art, design, or form compares with her beauty. She is unrivaled in purity, shrouded in mystery, born in the Dawn of time. She was created in the Eternal Garden, a daughter of Eve, matching those around her, a blossoming, eternal flower of attraction and life and light.

She is the bright star on the brow of humanity.

Unlike man, she is not utilitarian. She is no workhorse or knotted old tree stump. She was not created as a block of muscle and bone. She has form and delicate shape. She is curves and hips, soft skin and bright lips. Even more than her body, her soul is beauty. The lights in her eyes dazzle when she smiles. And the world stops to notice.

J. R. R. Tolkien finds the best description of this magic—this Garden magic—in *The Silmarillion*. He shows this enchantment in the epic love of Beren for Lúthien. Beren, a man, is the warrior and resistance leader against the Dark Enemy; Lúthien, the elfish princess, is fairest of creatures under the moon. Tolkien recalls their first meeting:

> It is told...that Beren came stumbling into Doriath, grey and bowed as with many years of woe, so great had been the torment of the road. But wandering in the summer in the woods...he came upon Lúthien...at a time of evening under moonrise, as she danced upon the unfading grass in the glades...Then all memory of his pain departed from him, and he fell into an enchantment; for Lúthien was the most beautiful of all the Children of Ilúvatar. Blue was her raiment as the unclouded heaven, but her eyes were grey as the starlit evening; her mantle was sewn with golden flowers, but her hair was dark as the shadows of twilight. As the light upon the leaves of trees, as the voice of clear waters, as the stars above the mists of the world, such was her glory and her loveliness; and in her face was a shining light.

But she vanished from his sight; and he became dumb, as one that is bound under a spell, and he strayed long in the woods, wild and wary as a beast, seeking for her. In his heart he called her Tinúviel, that signifies Nightingale, daughter of twilight, in the Grey-elven tongue, for he knew no other name for her...

There came a time near dawn on the eve of spring, and Lúthien danced upon a green hill; and suddenly she began to sing. Keen, heart-piercing was her song as the song of the lark that rises from the gates of night and pours its voice among the dying stars, seeing the sun behind the walls of the world; and the song of Lúthien released the bonds of winter, and the frozen waters spoke, and flowers sprang from the cold earth where her feet had passed.

Then the spell of silence fell from Beren, and he called to her.[1]

When the mystic woman dances on the green hills before us, *we notice.*

Like Beren, we fall perilously under her spell. We are beautifully ruined.

When she notices us in return, our deep soul is aroused. There is a stirring in us, a body hunger. This may make us nervous or guilty, as it awakens our sexual prowess and desire. Our sexual desire which was created *good.* Even if it makes the uninitiated man or the religious crowd uneasy, this pure enchantment is good.

Deeply good.

Unfortunately, it was twisted—like all things—in the Fall.

Some twist, reduce, and pervert the feminine image for profit. This is abusive and exploitive manipulation. It is a corruption of Eden, a perversion of pure beauty, and a cosmic tragedy. Even worse, millions willingly bite into the apple, creating a "market demand" for it.

The lie of the pornographic image speaks indiscriminately into oblivion, seducing anyone who will listen. Its open-ended invitation is for everyone and no one. Despite what it promises, the enchantment is not exclusive. The image has no feelings or care or specificity. This is the subtle lie of the virtual siren. She sings her tune, offering ecstasy in her sweet and forbidden morsels. Our soul hears and delights:

You have aroused me, which makes you powerful.
My desire for you says you are wanted.
You are sexual and strong.

The siren's call is a promise of herself and her body. She offers affirmation, promising to answer our deep man questions, the questions of our own sexual prowess. By giving ourselves to her, we believe our deep soul thirst will be quenched.

Gripped with rabid madness, we drink deeply of lust, worshipping her body for sustenance, for life. We hunger for her, for her webs of her enchantment, but she is not ours to have. She is an illusion. We move toward her as one does a mirage, sailing blindly and without heed, until we break upon the stone.

Like the Corinthians, we visit the Temple of Aphrodite, worship her breasts, and give ourselves away to her prostitutes. We don't even leave the house to do this. We pick a virtual prostitute and spill out our life to her. But instead of finding the promised strength and sexual prowess, we are reduced to a loaf of a bread.

Unsatisfied, some of us bring the fantasy into real life, seeking nourishment. We—like the Corinthians—proclaim Christ but still worship the high places, and the altars of Aphrodite. Until we are caught, bitten deep by a steel-toothed trap, until the barbed arrow pieces our liver. We crash hard, lying facedown in the dirt, left for dead. Her seductions and sweet promises lead us down, down to the grave.

Others try to marry Mom.

We're attracted to strong women. We're at home in that narrative. We are used to being led, we grew up with that Mom story, and it's comforting. Comfort may even look like a bossy or overly controlling woman.

Mom was strong, responsible, and she took care of us. She paid the bills, paid the taxes, fixed the cars, bought groceries, made dinner. We are lost without her. So when we meet another woman similar to Mom, it feels like home.

We *know* her. So we marry her.

But once we do, we know something is amiss.

We're incapable of leading. So we untie Mom's rope from our waist, and hand it to our new leader, our wife. We expect her to pick up the rope, where Mom left off, but we're dumbfounded when she doesn't take it. "But this is what you are supposed to do..." we insist. "Take our rope! Do it now!"

We give control to her. She may take the rope, and even enjoy the control for a while. But ultimately she does not want to be our captain, or to be our mom.

Our wives, initially attracted to our receptiveness, now feel duped. They wanted us and now have us, but we have no viril-ity. We have no danger. No claws or fangs. We can feel her disappointment, so we try harder, giving her everything we can: obedience, loyalty, boyishness, humor, and playful affection. But since we've never found the wild masculine, we don't have it to offer.

Double frustration. She is frustrated and we are lost, incapable of bringing her what she needs. Instead we remain passive, receptive followers. Dormant. We were drawn into her positive energy, her life.

But now, we are *feeders*.

We ask our wife to carry our weight. Look to her for validation and affirmation. Our marriage feels like a question we're compelled to ask. It's also a question she is unable to answer. We're used to the doting tea ladies, who always say, "Yes, honey, that is sweet." We look to our wives for the same maternal pat on the head.

"Isn't this great, Mommy? Don't you like this?"

Even if she tries, our wife cannot answer our question.

When we got married, I asked my wife to answer my question.

I still didn't know who I was as a man. I had not yet found the wild masculine. I was indecisive, and didn't know how to fight clean or stand up for myself.

Before I was married, I allowed myself to be victimized by bosses—I was a passive receptor of everything they dished out. Since I was a man without boundaries or walls, bosses took advantage of me.

I did have a pure heart. I loved God and was a Christ follower, and had found some validation in my young career. Even though I had been through graduate school, I was still trying to take my first career steps. I was still searching, uncertain about my purpose and identity as a man.

I took my doubts to Kari. This led to countless hours of one-way conversations. I told her about my grief at work. My anger at bosses. I poured out complaints and dreams alike. She listened quietly and faithfully and patiently. She engaged, smiled, loved, and cared for me. She gave and gave and gave.

Unknowingly, I drained her with my selfishness.

It wasn't because I didn't love her or didn't want to please her. I worked my fingers to the bone for her. Mom loved me that way, and it's the only way I know how to love. But I still had an unanswered question, like a Black Mesa thorn, jammed deep in my soul—*am I a man?*

This question left me wearing blinders, unable to see how my doubts and insecurity dominated our conversations and marriage. I loved and served her relentlessly. Did thousands of dishes. Went on a thousand spontaneous dates. Bought her hand-made dresses. Surprised her with cards, flowers, and original art. I lavished her with gifts and worked hard to please her.

But I still missed it.

I still missed *her*, at the deep soul level.

I was unable to give her everything. My soul was unable to get past the questions that haunted me. Am I a man? Am I competent? Do I please you? What do you think of me? I never heard the answer and now I was desperately trying to get it from my wife. At the same time, she was *tired*.

My wife is arresting. She has a tender heart and gentle touch. She is an inviting hostess. And she is strong, from Nordic descent, with Viking blood. She could easily lead a boat full of rowdy Vikings. Spar with Wing Chun masters, or run a Fortune

500 company. She can (and has) developed urban community gardens, led nationally ranked dance classes, and run international law projects.

She has gifts and capacity and a work ethic. God built her that way.

But she is not built to carry me.

This is what I asked her to do. Whenever I asked, she didn't feel safe or wanted or loved. She grew frazzled and lonely. I grew depressed. Hopeless. I knew something was wrong with my marriage, but didn't know it was *me*. I was confused and conflicted.

I stopped working out, practicing karate, and playing flag football. Put on 40 pounds. Over time, I grew frustrated with her for not answering my man question. I even had the audacity to be frustrated with her. Looking back, I see how absurd it all was. A lot of men are frustrated because our wives refuse to be Mom.

News flash: *Our wives don't want to be our mom.*

She is not Mom. Or Dad. Or a tea lady.

She will never answer our question.

Many men quit, thinking the answer lies somewhere else, or it will never come. We get depressed, abuse drugs, or look at porn. Or we look for another woman who feels more like Mom.

These are lies and half-measures.

We're looking for something deeper, something a woman was not created to give. Our wife cannot call us into manhood, or lead us outside the beauty of the Garden. She can indirectly call us to manhood. She can listen to us as we dream about it. She can cheer for us as we awaken to it. She can stand with us on the edge of the Garden as we walk toward it—but she cannot take our steps—the steps assigned only to us.

Listen: A woman is magical but she is not your salvation.

Until we bring her true *wildness*—a masculine soul born outside of the Garden—both parties remain discontent. We are frustrated and our wives are unfulfilled. She's insecure, unsure about how we feel about her, how we can ever provide emotionally, spiritually, and physically. Robert Bly adds:

> A mother's job is to civilize the boy, so it's natural for her to keep the key. Attacking the mother, confronting her, shouting at her probably does not accomplish much—she may just smile and talk to you with her elbow on the pillow. The key has to be *stolen*. No woman worth her salt would give the key anyway. If a son can't steal it, he doesn't deserve it.[2]

I bought into the idea that I needed someone else to make me happy or fulfilled. Constantly. It's a lot like a victim mentality. "My dad wasn't around, so I'm not the man I could have been." "My wife won't answer my question, so I'll never know the answer." "My life depends on someone else to complete it."

We must burn those ideas to ashes.

Our journey starts with defiance.

Mom has a vision and a dream for us. It may be the right one and our God-ordained calling. Or, it may have to do with living in close proximity and leading safe lives. A good mom fights to protect her babies and keep them in the nest. Hell hath no fury like mama bear.

We know this. We have seen the protective fury of Mom and, perhaps, our wife. This is her job. Mom will never send us away. She will never tell us to go to the haunted woods or face the werebear. She doesn't like weapons. She is a preserver, and will visit us, even on death row. She will keep her wings around us, a faithful hen with her chicks. We need to see this and be grateful for Mom's protection, instead of acting like angry teenagers who shout at her.

But. We must defy Mom's protective will.

She will tell us not to go. She may even beg us. We must leave her nest.

We may think we leave Mom's nest when we go to college. Or get our first job. But inwardly, we still belong to her, like Max. Getting married might just be a transfer of ownership. Now our wife fights with Mom because it's unclear who holds the title.

Some of us need to stand up to Mom or their wife for the first time. Whatever standing up looks like, it never includes abuse, physical or mental harm. It is loving, but firm. It is truth wrapped in grace.

Others need to stop dating chain girlfriends, even if they scratch an itch. Like dogs, we roll over on our backs, asking them to scratch our bellies, and behind our ears. Like bull elks, we think we're more manly because we have a harem.

Others need to quit watching porn, whatever it takes. Even if this means taking aim with our Remington 870 at the computer screen. We need to stop asking a heartless image to answer our question. She always smiles and says we are sexual and strong. She's compliant, saying and doing anything we want her to do. She is everyone and no one, an objectification and dehumanization of true beauty. Millions believe she is real, but she is made of pixels.

We are getting played.

Most men need to confront themselves instead of Mom. We need to face our own codependency on her, find our own validation, and make our own decisions. What if we just quit asking for her approval—cold turkey? What if we lived and became the men we were called to be, no matter what anyone else said?

When we were boys, Mom was life.

This is normal. Mom nursed us. Gave us wisdom, protection. We listened to her. Sought her counsel. Wanted her acceptance. Mom helped us overcome stitches and algebra. Mom prayed us through storms and the dentist. Mom defended us from Something Awful, protected us from bullies and Roger Clemens.

Mom delivered us from the Wild Things.

But maybe the Wild Things are exactly what we need.

CHAPTER FIVE

The Wild Masculine

Our call is to the deep woods, away from
privacy fences, safety and control. We must face
Something Awful, stare him down, then return
home, changed.

We live far away from the woods, far away from the places of wildness. We've never walked the haunted pass, past the black pools of danger and trial, the overgrown places. We've steered clear of these. Our modern domestication has pushed the woods back to the lonely corners of our soul. To manicured patches on highway medians. To well-shorn hedges in the suburbs.

We are well scrubbed and wool suited. Trimmed and sanitized, groomed and pleasant to smell. Our modern, refined sensibilities are offended when we meet Romulus and Remus—the brothers raised by wolves—but they have something we do not. They have a certain danger, a secret life-giving wildness found only in the woods. And it takes this feral soul to create something great, like Rome.

W. H. Auden once said, "*A culture is no better than its woods.*"[1]

But what happens to the culture with no woods? It builds privacy fences. It has civility and manners. *Control.*

But it lacks the inherent danger and initiation rites necessary for boys to leave Mom and make for the hills, stare down Something Awful, then bring wildness back to the greater community.

There is something out there. Something dark and ferocious. Something covered with wet, tangled, and matted fur. Something waiting, and staring at us with black eyes and an open, fanged mouth.

Poet Robert Bly talks about this something lost in the hearts of men. Drawing from the Brothers Grimm German tale of *Iron*

John,[2] Bly says there's a large hairy man, Iron John, buried deep in our souls.

Iron John lives way out in the woods, buried at the bottom of a pond. When he does emerge from his pond, he is covered in reddish hair. No man who goes out to him returns. Anyone who walks too close to the pond gets pulled under by a hairy arm.

Men fear the *Hairy Man.*

Most are unwilling to go anywhere near his pond. We don't want to get pulled under and never heard from again. So the *Hairy Man* remains buried somewhere in the depths below, unseen and untouched.

Culture warns us against the *Hairy Man.*

It puts neon signs and fences around his pond. Whenever anyone brings out the *Hairy Man,* culture mocks him and binds him with chains, locking him away in an iron cage. Then, it gives the key into the keeping of the queen.

Culture pretends to like him, but only at a distance. He is amusement. They enjoy his peculiar beard, like him behind bars or on the television. He is entertainment, like the bearded men of *Duck Dynasty.*

Culture wishes for a milder, sweeter version: the safe man, the tame man, the shaved man, the emasculated man. Later, when Genghis Khan and his hordes come, culture bemoans, "Where have all the cowboys gone?"

The church, too, fears this image.

The longhaired Samson tearing apart a lion with his bare hands. The fiery Christ swinging a whip, flipping over tables and driving out moneychangers with holy anger. Or Josheb, a mighty man of David and chief of the Three, standing against eight hundred enemies and *killing them all with his spear.*

These images make us nervous. And rightly so.

Perhaps it's because we equate the *Hairy Man* with the *Savage Man*. This conjures up images of the criminal, the abuser, the dead-beat dad. We think of the rapist, or the destructive force who abuses his family, invades countries, uses WMD, traffics children, and wrecks havoc on society. Culture and the church rightly lock away the *Savage Man*.

It's easy to confuse the two. After all, the *Hairy Man* has the same wild look in his eyes. His hands are leathery. He smells like raw earth. He has a dangerous, even terrible, burning look. He cannot be controlled, coaxed, or manipulated. He simmers with the white-hot fires of quiet intensity; he radiates a pulsing and living strength.

The *Hairy Man* is no mindless savage or barbarian. He's not Vlad the Impaler. Far from it. He is—in the words of Mr. Beaver—"not a tame lion. But he is good." The *Hairy Man* represents our strength. Our sexuality.

He represents the *wild masculine*.

I searched for the wild masculine among the Kodiak bears of Alaska.

A couple months earlier, my dad called and asked to go on an adventure. It was a generous offer, but it also made me nervous. As an adult, I'd never been on a trip with him. Before Kodiak, all my adult time with Dad was in flashes and snippets; it could be measured in minutes and hours, not weeks.

Needless to say, when he offered to take me on a trip, I was apprehensive. He mentioned going to Kenya to watch the Maasai Mara animal migration, to see the Big Five, and interact with the Maasai people.

The Maasai are a tribe in Kenya and Northern Tanzania. The

Maasai men are raised to be warriors, wearing red and carrying tribal shields and spears. Maasai males do not marry when they are young; instead, they are circumcised at fourteen, then spend eight years out in the wild tending the flocks. Traditionally, the boys hunted and killed a lion with a spear.

They become men on the return trip back to the village.

So when my dad offered a trip to visit Kenya, to see the lions and leopards and meet the Maasai, it sounded amazing. I told him I wanted to go.

For the next few months, he e-mailed and asked me what I was thinking. Then, after several violent political clashes near our destination, Dad called the trip off. It was the right call.

I felt this was partly my fault. Even though there was violence and unrest in Nairobi, I couldn't help feeling partly to blame for the cancellation, as I'd dragged my feet with the preparations. After Dad canceled, I called him and told him I would love to go with him on a safari somewhere else.

I suggested Kodiak Island.

He agreed.

So we bought our plane tickets and went.

Surrounded by the ocean, Kodiak Island represents a special sort of wildness even for Alaska. It is ringed by active volcanoes, and is a jagged piece of rugged land. It is foreboding and inhospitable to travelers, photographers, and especially, the flower-shirted *Mickey-Mouse-Ear-Wearing Tourist Guy.*

It's nearly impossible to get to Kodiak. You can hitch a ride on the back of a killer whale. Or you can fly to Homer, then take the eight-hour boat ride. Or you can try to fly direct. I flew.

After we boarded the plane, they took my suitcase off, without telling me, and left it in Anchorage. It would have to arrive the next day. The plane weighed too much. Just a week earlier, an overloaded small plane had crashed and killed fifteen people.

The dense fog made the whole island invisible. Our pilot was unable to land, and had to pull up hard twice, then circle back, as the runway goes straight into a mountain. On our second pass, we cleared the mountain by five hundred feet. The local attorney sitting beside me had his face in his hands. On the final pass, we saw the runway about fifty feet aboveground. The pilot landed the plane to a standing ovation.

After landing on the island, we took another seaplane—a Beaver—an hour flight over the green lakes and the mountains. There are not many roads on Kodiak, only the main roads around the city, so everyone travels on seaplanes.

It was good to see my half brother, Chris, who I've seen only a handful of times in my life. He grew up on a ranch in Amarillo, Texas, and is at home in the wild. He is a competitor like me, and he likes facial hair. Chris has lived all over the world, so it was cool to compare travel notes. Kodiak was our first man-trip together. We crawled on our bellies through the mud and the muck and the tall grass. Good times.

It was good to connect with dad.

I grew up hunting ducks and deer, with mentors and friends, but Kodiak was our first "hunt" together. I found a six-foot branch of driftwood and gave it to him for a walking stick. He used it to cross the streams. He pointed out bald eagles and some sea otters splashing in the bay. That afternoon, he caught a massive halibut.

Not a lot was said, but we were *together*. We were on level footing, away from hindrances and distractions. These were huge moments.

After our hike, he saw me typing on my MacBook and asked what I was doing. I told him I was trying to write a book on manhood, but it was a slippery and treacherous endeavor. I was just trying to figure it out. I told him it wasn't a macho book, as much as my learning journey. I read him a paragraph.

We talked about Hemingway, his favorite author. He could write a good story using very few words. One time, he was challenged to write one in six words or less. After thinking for a few moments, he wrote on a napkin:

For sale: baby shoes. Never worn.

Back at the lodge, Mike, who was our guide, had guns everywhere. Guns on his walls, over the door, the fireplace mantel, in the gun case. High-powered rifles. Ancient shotguns. Huge .454 pistols.

Dad and I talked about the guns. We asked Mike about each one. They all had stories. Family stories. Bear stories. We talked about the different calibers necessary for large game, like bears. We talked about shot placement. Bolt action versus semi-auto.

Writing and guns were safe topics. They were default conversations, safe areas of common ground. Sitting there in the Kodiak wilds, a thousand miles from nowhere, I felt like I needed to say something more. I needed to say something deeper, more meaningful or profound. But words escaped me.

I'm not sure many men go off the deep end in conversations.

I'm sure it gets deep sometimes, but I don't really see men crying together over a baby name, the latest romance novel, or the perfect dahlia bloom. Even though Dad and I failed to get to the deep end, our talks were good. They were a start.

The next morning, Dad woke us up at four. Chris rolled over and groaned. I pretended to be asleep. The way Dad was acting,

I thought a bear was trying to steal our beer. After much effort, I stumbled to the window and saw two spotted fawns playing outside the window, along the beach. Dad loved watching them. I watched for a moment or two, then dragged myself back to bed.

Camp was a tangled, overgrown thing. Five-foot-tall ferns. Whale vertebrae strewn along the path. A sun-bleached moose skull and antlers greeted us at the cabin door. No phone reception, no lights or electricity, except for a few brief hours at night by generator. Bears often strolled through camp, a few feet from the cabins, to drink from the stream. Because of the tall brush, a bear could be five feet away, lying in the ferns, and you would never know.

Unlike my modern and civilized life, where domestication has pushed the woods to the brink of extinction, Kodiak is the opposite. Wildness has kept civilization at bay; it is the people who are secondary. People live on the edges, on the beaches, on cliff faces and the fringes of the island. Westward expansion is limited.

The Kodiak bear is the soul of the island. He lives only on the island, is a distant cousin of the grizzly, and is the largest bear in the world. The first one I met was nearly eleven feet tall, a 1,500-pound brute, standing in the lobby of the lodge.

His eyes and ears are keen; his nose is better than a bloodhound's. Arms longer and thicker than my legs, and he has a fist full of six-inch, hooked claws. He bites harder than a steel bear trap, and he can break an elk's neck with *one swipe*.

He is the perfect hunter. Dangerous. Fearless. Unstoppable.

I was not able to take a gun or bear pepper spray, but I knew I needed *something*. Something in case we had a personal and up-close connection. Fighting him was an unlikely and foolish proposition. I would have little or no chance against a Kodiak, but I still needed something. Something I could put my hands on and grip tightly.

I needed a knife.

I did research, visited a knife and gun show, and finally decided on a Bowie. It was heavy, strong, and had a stout eight-inch blade. It was designed for military operatives. Even with the knife, I knew a confrontation weighed heavily in favor of the Kodiak. At least I wouldn't be an easy hors d'oeuvre. So I bought the knife, tested it, modified the grip, and then packed it away in my backpack.

Something felt wrong about buying one.

It felt as if a sage, a reclusive warrior, or an old master should give me a knife. Someone wise, someone far down the road ahead of me, someone I looked up to and respected immensely. Someone like Black Elk, the mystic. Or one of his Lakota descendants, my late friend Richard Twiss.

Richard was a visionary, a prophet, and a healer. He wore his hair in long braids sitting on his shoulders. He was quick witted and humble, seeking to be "the common man." We need more men like Richard.

In my mind, I could see Richard drifting along on the banks of the Columbia River at dawn. He emerges from the mists, smiling. He walks toward me, and hands me a powerful talisman, a knife, to aid me against the dark things.

In that spirit, I sought out a master to teach me how to make one.

I learned how to make a knife using Damascus steel—a method of blade making that was developed in the Ancient Near East. Traditionally, Damascus blades are forged together from different types of steel, by folding and layering steel and iron, up to five hundred times.

I worked with a metalworker to forge steel, and then took it to my workshop. Put it under the grinder, cooled it, heat-treated it, and gave it a razor edge. I drilled holes in the tang and attached the handle.

I named it *Mato*—Lakota for "bear."

I'm not sure why I was compelled to seek out the Kodiak. But whatever it was, it was something primal. The Kodiak is the symbol for the great unseen things of my imagination—the Wild Things. Massive and unyielding, he is bigger than the full moon. Hidden in the shrubs, the tall grass and ferns, he waits—a giant shadow upon the earth.

I wanted to find him and stare him down. To stand with him, face-to-face, and confront him. Maybe all this sounds insane. Maybe it is.

But I think seeking him was about me inviting the wildness. Standing up to it, without fear, and in some way, *bringing it back within me*. I searched because I never felt a sense of masculine initiation. I never felt fully like a man. Now I was hunting for the Kodiak bear, and for peace with a man I wanted to know better, my father.

I wasn't sure how to hunt for either.

Or what I was supposed to do once I found them.

I do know the wild masculine doesn't live at home, inside stainless steel kitchen appliances or behind white picket fences. He's not sleeping on my couch, putting his feet on my coffee table, watching Hulu.

The *Hairy Man* doesn't live inside with Mom.

He's somewhere else. Far from home and familiarity—he's outside.

Whatever I'm looking for is lurking in the deep woods.

On Kodiak, I was itching to get out, but Mike was in no hurry. He was calm. Unruffled. He knew the bears would be there, waiting for us. Mike was born on Kodiak and spent his entire life off the grid. His demeanor was refreshing. Counter to the bravado pride found in so many self-proclaimed "tough guys." Even though he hunts world-record bears for a living, Mike is reserved. Humble even. He quietly goes about his business. He's a patient listener, and doesn't have to have the last word.

When I peppered him with hunting questions, he talked about himself for only a bit, then changed the subject, putting the focus back on us. Even though Mike lives off the grid, climbs mountains with a fifty-pound backpack, and stalks record-book bears for a living, he never once bragged or acted like "the expert."

The first morning, we loaded up the boat and listened as its twin diesel engines churned and hummed, motoring us down the still river, into the great unseen.

Salmon were jumping everywhere. The silvers were spawning, returning from the sea to the freshwater steams. Swimming and fighting upstream. Looking for their exact birthplace, to lay their eggs and die. Two or three years out to sea, and then they return, bodies slapping against the water, small claps against the morning stillness.

White-manned bald eagles dotted the tree line. Hunting. Watching with keen eyes, the eagle spots his prey up to a mile away. Glides out to meet it with his seven-foot wingspan, catching salmon and seagull chicks.

After an hour boat ride, we were dropped off on a rocky beach, on the edge of the woods. We walked single-file behind Mike. He whispered and told us to keep our voices down and to stay close, not to wander off. We were to move as ghosts, gliding silently across the beach and into the tall grass. It was just us, the eagles, the gulls, and a lonely harbor seal barking off in the distance.

It wasn't long before we saw a patch of brown, a glimpse of a huge Kodiak lumbering off into the tree line. He was obscured by the brush, but his bulk was obvious, easily over 1,000 pounds. He slooped off and walked away calmly, vanishing into the shadows and the mist.

A few hours later, a sow and her two cubs worked their way toward us.

She was large and had a shiny blond coat. Sows can be very dangerous and aggressive, especially with cubs in tow. Mike let us know that we shouldn't get too close to her, as he was once forced to kill a large sow in the very spot we were standing. Someone accidentally surprised her, lying down in the tall grass, and she attacked without warning. Mike killed her at six feet.

This sow got within fifty yards of us before we slowly stood out from the grass, letting her know we were near. She veered off— kept walking toward us, but angled away slightly. We had several more encounters like this.

On the last day, we got close to a massive bear.

We saw it in the tall grass, so we circled downwind, trying to intercept. The grass was taller than we were so we were walking blindly, but carefully, in its direction. I saw it on the edge of a creek, about fifty yards away. We bowed our heads below the grass and inched forward. Slowly.

As we got near the creek, the grass was shorter. We crawled on hands and knees the last ten yards. The bear was in the act of catching a salmon. Like a huge brown cat jumping on a yarn ball, it pounced, thrusting its front arms and head underwater.

Seconds later, it scooped the fish up with two massive paws, clamped down on it, then proudly carried it to the bank. We sat there motionless, listening to it crunch salmon bones. Nothing between us and the bear but a few blades of grass. The bear was so close I could smell it—it stank, like a wet dog, with dank, muddy fur.

Suddenly, the bear stood up—a full nine feet tall—and looked right at us.

We froze.

I met its gaze.

And smiled.

After a tense few moments, the bear dropped down and went back to eating.

We watched her for a while longer and then slipped away.

Something mystical happens in those moments. Your breathing gets shallow. Adrenaline. You feel a heightened sense of things. Vision and hearing become more acute. You feel stronger.

Then, an internal fortitude comes.

A stillness. A slowing down. A welcoming.

When Death smiles at you and you smile back, *something changes*.

This is an explosive moment.

A threshold moment. This moment can anchor your soul when the locusts come, or when the plague claims your livestock. It will tether you to the masts, bracing you against the sirens.

For the rest of your life, you will draw water from the well of this moment. Once you face death, other problems don't matter as much. The cold rain no longer affects you—now you welcome the weather on your face. Everything else in your life feels smaller. Challenges sure, but ones you can *deal with*:

- The baby that needs a diaper change or a milk bottle.
- The lady that cuts you off in the grocery line.
- The bicyclist that gives you the finger.
- The barista who screws up your latte.

These things now seem trivial. Before, they got you irritated, ruffled, and upset, but they don't matter anymore. Sure, they make you raise your eyebrows, but now they're just pesky flies on the back of the bear.

The day I left Kodiak, I asked Mike what it meant to be a man.

We crawled through mud together. Stalked bears in the long grass—got so close that I could smell them. We hiked miles inland to fish for salmon and Dolly Varden. We caught and fried halibut and drank local cider together.

Mike's life matched the wild rhythm of the island.

So when he told me what a man was, I listened.

"To me, being a man means being kind, generous, and a good provider. The most important part of being a man is being strong. Having the self-confidence to handle any situation you face, whether you live in the city and face traffic, congestion, and crowds, or you live in remote areas with wild animals and inclement weather. And it's a quiet self-confidence. A strong, self-confident man doesn't announce his strength to the world. He leads by example. He's the guy who steps up and takes charge when a challenge is faced, and then quietly fades into the background when the issue is resolved."

Once you face the bear, you no longer have anything to prove.

You relax and ease into quiet confidence. You're not worried about your gear, your hairstyle, or the posers in the softball league. You no longer feel like a poser. And you don't even judge those poser guys anymore; you're just quiet around them.

Facing the wilderness helps you face your own inadequacy when it comes to fixing stuff. Before, you were intimidated by the lawn mower. The weed-eater. Organizing the garage. Before, you looked to others for help.

Now, you welcome the fires of the forge.

You welcome obstacles as challenges. The Kodiak is your opportunity.

You are changed. Your knuckles are hardened. A quiet fire burns somewhere deep within—an inner ferocity waiting, ready to rise up against the dark things. You are calmer now, but more dangerous. Grim, but with a greater capacity for joy.

Your senses are now honed razors, sharpened by Arkansas black whetstone. Your once-boyish eyes have turned gray—and hawkish. The air tastes cleaner. You are no longer afraid to cry. Or roar. Or dance in the streets. The *Hairy Man* no longer dwells deep at the bottom of a pond, *he is right under your skin.*

"Wildness," according to Martin Shaw, "is a form of sophistication, because it carries a true knowledge of our place in the world. It doesn't exclude civilization, but prowls through it. It knows when to attend to the needs of the committee, and when to drink from the moonlit lake. It wears a suit when it has to, but refuses to trim its talons or whiskers. It is not afraid of emotion, of grief forests and triumphant returns."[3]

Something Awful is still out there.

But he doesn't dominate your life anymore.

You look forward to confronting him, even if all you have is a knife. The feral spirit you bring home from the dark woods is light for others. It is a fiery brew, awakening all who partake.

Most men keep their distance. But for the brave few who drink, your blood-colored elixir gives life; builds families, homes, and cities; and invites others to venture out into the wild.

The last day on Kodiak, we loaded up our small Beaver Seaplane. It could only hold 1,500 pounds, so we carefully weighed the luggage and ourselves. Mike stood on the rickety, bleached-wooden pier, watching us. This was his quiet way of saying good-bye.

We took off low across the water, barely clearing the trees. We flew over snow-capped peaks, over white mountain goats and the elusive *Mato*.

I looked out across the jagged peaks, satisfied. I had faced something. Confronted something. More than a treacherous hike or a massive bear—I had faced myself.

We grow when we face ourselves. When we confront Something Awful. When we summon the courage to take on the impossible, venture into the haunted woods and step into the nourishing dark.

It was hard to leave Kodiak; it felt like I was leaving something behind. I wanted to stay and soak in the wildness, but I needed to return. Poet Galway Kinnell put words on my grizzled soul when he said:

I know that I love the day,
The sun on the mountain, the Pacific
Shiny and accomplishing itself in breakers,
But I know I live half alive in the world,
Half my life belongs to the wild darkness.[4]

CHAPTER SIX

The Mythic Path

Our way to the wild masculine follows the One
True Myth.

My heart awoke in the wildness of Alaska. I didn't understand it at the time, but I brushed up against something more powerful than a bear. Something ancient and deep and pulsing and rhythmic. It felt like a living thing—it felt like *initiation*.

These ancient rhythms: Leaving home, getting off the grid, staring down the Kodiak, changed me. They were what I needed, what my soul hunted for. There was something substantive, something wild and alive, that I brought back with me. Thoreau was right when he said, "We need the tonic of wildness."[1]

Many have never tasted this tonic. We have no draughts of wildness to press against our lips. No wells, springs, or rivers to drink from with cupped hands. Young men are usually invited to drink by an elder. But we have no elders. No initiation rites. No place.

We have no clear road or definition of manhood.

We don't even have *language* for it.

We look to Mom, but she is busy warning us about the woods. "You'll put your eye out," she scolds. We look to pop culture, and find exaggerations or ridicules of masculinity. Without a lantern, the wild places feel forbidden. Dangerous. We may summon the courage to wander out into the woods, but we have no road markers. No sense of direction. No map.

We wonder: "*Am I a man?*"

But the answer is a moving target.

Even at thirty or forty or fifty, we may feel and act *boyish*.

Our friends tell us we become a man when we lose our

virginity. Have our first fistfight. Make a million dollars. Mom says we become men when we graduate college, get a job, and settle down. Culture says manhood is not trustworthy or is irrelevant. Gender is a choice—men may become women and vice versa, based on whim or feeling. Children take hormone therapy if they feel like a "boy" or a "girl" trapped inside.

We are tragically lost.

Our journey forward follows an ancient path; it follows the Kodiak Way.

We find it by crawling through the ferns and tall grass, over the green chamomile plants and eagle feathers. We move toward it by wading through the streams and scanning the ground for massive, five-toed tracks. When we find a fresh trail and track it, we brush into something more powerful than any creature.

Unwittingly, I tapped into movement, into rhythms—found in ancient stories, in legends and myths. Historically, these rhythms were told and sung and shared around sacred campfires passed down from generations of elders to younger men. These rhythms are sometimes found in our modern stories. They illuminate our lost path of initiation. They are flickering torches, throwing broken light on our steps.

But our journey is more than make-believe. It is more than imagination, more than fairy tale. This is our life—our living myth. Rumi invites us: "Don't be satisfied with stories, how things have gone with others. Unfold your own myth."[2] Legend and myth have happened, but myth is also happening now.

Myth exists in this very moment, all around us, in the 360-degree circle surrounding our lives. Myth is something told with words and song, but myth is also something we carry, something we create.

Deep within us, every man longs for initiation. He longs to go into the Kodiak woods, drink the tonic of wildness, face Something Awful, and then return to the mainland—changed. We long to test ourselves, to push and break our limits. We are restless to break the expectations placed on us by others, find the wild masculine, and step into the myth ourselves. Many of us already have. Others have made the "prestep" in our imagination.

The mythic path can only be seen through eyes of wonder.

But not everyone is a fan of myth.

Some believe myth belongs only to the childish worlds of Disney and Pixar. The idea of myth as something containing truth is completely foreign or ridiculous. Myth has lost its sacred place in our culture. Today, the word "myth" is synonymous for "lie." It is no longer a compass or guide for initiation; it now belongs to Mickey Mouse.

Our culture agrees with atheist Jack Lewis, who once told his friend John, "Myths are lies and therefore worthless, even though breathed through silver."[3]

To which John replied, "*No. They are not lies.*"

"We have come from God," John continued, "and myths woven by us contain error. But they also reflect a splintered fragment of the true light, the eternal truth that is with God. Only by myth making, only by becoming 'sub-creators' and inventing stories, can man aspire to the state of perfection he knew before the Fall. Our myths may be misguided but they steer us shakily towards the true harbor."

The two men talked until 3:00 a.m.

When they finally returned home, John "J. R. R." Tolkien wrote his friend a poem. And Jack "C. S." Lewis converted from atheist to Christ-follower. Tolkien later wrote:

"In the Gospels, legend and history have met and fused. Art has been verified. God is the Lord of angels, and of men, and—of elves."[4]

That night in Oxford, I walked closely behind Tolkien and Lewis. I listened as they argued about myth. I agreed with Tolkien much faster than Lewis. As Tolkien said, myth is a "splintered fragment" and a "cracked compass," I nodded. I realized Tolkien and King Solomon are both right: "God has set eternity in the heart of every man" (Ecclesiastes 3:11).

Suddenly, I saw a distant light.

Could myth steer me toward the wild masculine?

What if the mythic storytellers, who came from diverse backgrounds, cultures, languages, and time periods, were all hitting on the same thing? What if they were hearing the same timeless, initiation rhythms? Even more, what if these rhythms had divine echoes, and originated with God?

What does this mean?

Our way to the wild masculine follows the one true Myth.

These rhythms—these mythic steps—were road markers in the life of Jesus, the Incarnate God Man. He moved from being the Son of Mary to the Son of the Father. He left the village and went under the river, and then into the wilderness. He returned to heal and teach for three years, then entered Jerusalem on a donkey with his eyes fixed on the Skull. Defeating death, he came back and stepped into the Risen Beyond.

The way to the wild masculine follows the wind trails of Jesus as he walked into manhood, as he was called, initiated, empowered, and sent by the Father.

This is the heroic path.

It starts with leaving the comforts of Mom's house. We head outdoors, to the river, and meet a *Hairy Man* named John. Then, empowered with a talisman, we enter the wilderness to confront ourselves and the Enemy. After our fight, we are transformed and return to the village, changed.

- Severance
- Confrontation
- Transformation
- Return

The mythic steps.

They show us the long-buried path of masculine initiation.

Our path begins with **severance**.

This is an intentional leaving. This is getting up and breaking free to make the change. Severance is an internal move before anything else. According to Eudora Welty, "all serious daring starts from within."

Severance is also *right now*.

There is immediacy and finality to it. There is no going back.

This is Morpheus handing us the red pill. This is Bilbo, then later Frodo, leaving the Shire. This is Odysseus taking a ship to the Underworld. This is Theseus flying the black sail on the way to the Minotaur's labyrinth. This is Luke leaving Tatooine with Obi-Wan, then later going to Dagobah.

Severance presents opportunity but does not linger long at our door.

We hear its faint knocking, but if we roll over, cross our arms, and go back to sleep, it is gone in the morning. Most men just roll over. Slip back into normalcy. Severance requires waking up, daring, and even recklessness. We must open the door, join the pirates on the black corsair, and sail toward dawn.

I learned something about severance by watching the coho salmon on Kodiak. There is a primal instinct, an unknown song moving these little warrior fish. They leave home, go hundreds of miles out to sea, and a few years later, come back. Back to the fresh waters, to the place of their birth, to spawn, give new life, and die.

Men are born with the coho instinct.

Some obey the inner coho stirring, break loose, seek danger and life. Many others remain at home or lost at sea. Every man feels it, beginning in his teenage years. But with no pirates around to call him to the docks, the young man remains stuck. Most young men don't recognize this mythic stirring, but we feel it. Red aggression. Sexual urges. Growing strength.

Our bodies want to *move*.

Military ads are wisely aimed at this stirring. They promise action. Jumping out of helicopters, emerging from water with painted faces and M16s. For the man gripped by the stirring, life moves too slow. For this man, sitting in a classroom or cubicle feels painful. He is a bristling, wolfish creature, looking for purpose and a pack.

Storytellers often send heroes into the woods for initiation. We must head out and find our direction magnetically. Sometimes the woods come to us. This is Anodos, who wakes up to find his room has been transformed into a forest. Beethoven once wrote, *"It seems as if every tree said to me: 'Holy! Holy!' Who can give complete expression to the ecstasy of the woods?"*[5]

Whatever the mechanics, our severance rhythm is the same.

We see the coho stirring in the twelve-year-old Jesus, who stays behind in the temple for three days. This was a key year, as it was his *bar mitzvah*, the year he became "son of the commandment." Jesus stays behind asking questions, learning, listening. Joseph and Mary miss him for two days. When they finally find him, they are rightly anxious. Jesus says to them: "Don't you know I must be in my Father's house?" (Luke 2:49).

I believe Jesus feels the mythic stirring, the call to the wild masculine. He begins to identify less as the Son of Mary and more as the Son of the Father. He is still eighteen years away from launching out into mission, but he begins the move at twelve. Like Christ, our severance begins with leaving Mom and moving toward the Father's house.

But many men never leave the village.

Manhood knocks at the drawbridge of our soul. We may flee, repress, or ignore this knocking. It takes real courage to lower the gate and step across the invisible boundary. Our severance call is like the fabled newspaper ad rumored to be placed by Ernest Shackleton in the early 1900s seeking adventurers to join one of his expeditions to the South Pole:

Men wanted for hazardous journey. Low wages, bitter cold. Long months of complete darkness, constant danger. Safe return doubtful. Honor and recognition in the event of success.

Many men are called but few go. The rare one returns. Some men return but don't offer anything back to the greater community. But if we do manage to make it to the blizzards of the South Pole, we cross an invisible barrier.

This is our *threshold moment*.

This is past the point of no return. Something drastic and life altering happens. We find a dragon's egg and then it hatches. The goblins have come and burned the village. The threshold moment may be spending your savings to launch your dream. Or leaving a crowd of rubbish friends behind. Deciding you will no longer live as a victim. Moving to another city to find a new life.

Once we cross the threshold, we must go forward, like it or not.

It's hard to say when we actually cross the invisible barrier.

This is why it's important to keep our ear to the ground, listening to the Spirit's call. Many men launch out to do great things, with great enthusiasm, spending great resources on things that are fleeting. Many waste years of time and millions of dollars with the best intentions, creating nonprofits and foundations and churches and hospitals. This is the danger of self-willed severance.

Severance is not whipping ourselves up into a frenzy and then setting out to do something great. It requires patience. It is more like the call of the prophet Samuel. We wait and listen for the quiet call of the Spirit. Then, when we do hear its whisper, we activate as servants, listening and moving decisively, plowing forward without looking back.

Along the way, a mentor or an elder may be involved. Sometimes we meet him before our severance, sometimes after. Like the biblical Eli, to go lie down, and be receptive to God's call.

In our culture, there is a serious lack of elders.

When fathers willfully abandon a generation, it leaves millions of boys lost. When fathers leave not for war or courage or self-sacrifice, but for convenience and self-interest, it shakes the village. Boys are stuck trying to sort out the coho stirring by themselves. The results, like *Lord of the Flies*, are tragic.

Historically, the Circle of Elders lead us away from our mother's house. They stand at the edge of the village, beating the war drums and calling us out. The drums are our signal. It is time to leave Mom and move off into the deep woods. Once we are in the woods, they speak into our lives and teach us wisdom. Like Jethro, the father-in-law of Moses, elders show us how to navigate the high seas.

An elder often steps in right before an epic fail. He breaks us from the village, helping us step over the threshold. He gives us a talisman, a protective ward against the dark. The talisman takes many forms. A Mithril vest. A singing bow. A bear-claw pendant. A lightning spear. Whatever he gives us, it prepares us for the coming fight.

Elders show us the next mythic step, which is always **confrontation**.

In the haunted woods, we are put to the test. We must face the yellow eyes. Hunt werewolves. Climb down the well to face the demon who lies below. Or confront our dark father, who is now a Sith Lord.

Sometimes, there are multiple confrontations.

As with every confrontation, there is fear and, usually, a chance to escape. We may avoid the fight altogether. There is a real chance of failure. Pain is guaranteed. Our fear is bound to the pain, bound to our possible death. We know the fight *will* be painful, so we avoid it and wander aimlessly in the woods. When we avoid confrontation, we remain untested and unsure of our strength.

Confrontation may be a life-and-death proposition.

There are horizontal confrontations, like standing up to a boss or a coworker, a spouse or our parents. For the passive man or the victim man, this is a difficult challenge. These men have no edges or boundaries, and their posture habitually allows other people to victimize them. When trials come, these men habitually roll over on their backs and apologize. Their confrontation begins with building healthy walls and standing upright.

Our fight may be facing that which keeps us depressed, lonely, addicted, or cynical. It may start with a simple, angry denial, a holy discontent at the state of things. Then it is anchored by the firm resolution that life must get better.

Some men overcompensate, like *Gym Guy*, determined to prove their strength to everyone and themselves. But surface bravado does not root a man. When danger comes, he goes AWOL, flees, or becomes a deserter. Like Jonah, he grabs the first boat to Tarshish. He may posture and puff, but inside, he lives in fear. He may leave his family and his comrades when things get dicey. This is not the man you want to lock arms with when Xerxes sends his Immortals.

Along with horizontal fights, there are also vertical, spiritual confrontations.

We see Christ begin his spiritual fight in the wilderness, east of the River Jordan. Even though he is famished, he relies on the Spirit in his confrontation with the Enemy.

Christ has earthly skirmishes—confronting greedy and wicked religious leaders, crashing their party. He confronts and overturns the tables of the Pharisees in the Temple. Again, he faces his fear in the Garden and then walks toward his final confrontation at the Skull.

Our spiritual confrontation begins with ourselves. No matter what we think, what we say, pretend, imagine, or fashion, we have self-destructive tendencies—and we all face death. There is no going around it. Like the second son, Cain, self-destruction crouches at our door, waiting to devour us. If we submit to it, we fall short of our destiny, hurt ourselves and others, and reap the bitter harvest. Eventually, it kills us.

But we are called to master it. The only way for us to survive is by facing our mortality, and surrendering it into the capable hands of another.

If we survive our mythic confrontation, there is **transformation**.

Something changes when we face the bear, when we face our own mortality. Once we face our worst nightmare, nothing else seems as daunting. Once we confront our darkest fears, we can face anything else. We no longer have to convince ourselves that we're not afraid. Fear still exists but has lost its grip. It will be back, but the confrontation and transformation stands as a steel H-beam, bracing us against the storm.

The men who live through confrontations exude quiet strength.

They don't have to prove it on Twitter or Facebook, or by being the guy who "one-ups" everyone else at parties. When you're around them, they feel less like a pro-wrestler wannabe and more like Mike, my Kodiak guide. There is something settling, something calming about him.

People usually can't describe this type of strength, but they can feel it.

There is something trustworthy about this man. It's not that he never makes mistakes, but you can count on him. Others look to him for guidance or wisdom. Even without seeing his résumé or job title or social media pedigree, they sense his fortitude.

The uninitiated man often lives in constant competition, trying to prove his strength and worth to others and to himself. He derides other men and is a cynic, tearing down and belittling, living in envy of others' success. At the heart of this man are fear and a lack of initiation. This man has never found his strength, and tries desperately to posture himself above others, convincing himself he has it.

For years, I had vivid dreams about fighting battles.

My friend Nick called these my Braveheart dreams. I saw images of riding and shooting out of the back of a pickup truck, postapocalypse style. Or swinging a sword, defending my family and taking out the bad guys. I was amazed at the power and emotion behind these dreams and how the images stuck with me.

As I grew older and graduated from college, the dreams grew stronger and more intense. It wasn't until I stopped and thought and prayed about it that I realized these dreams represented my *buried strength*.

There were confrontations I avoided and needed to face. For years, my heart and soul felt like a twitchy racehorse, a powerful Thoroughbred just before the dash. I knew I would keep having these dreams until I faced my fears and found my strength.

The ancient elders knew this when they created various initiation rites. They knew a boy's strength must be released, unlocked, and embraced. We, like the great horses, were created to run. The rites are simply a way to open the gates.

The elders knew we needed to face our mortality. They knew

it is only after we face the yellow eyes of death that we can run at breakneck speed toward life. The confrontation usually costs us.

We live through our fight, but we lose something. It involves sacrifice. Like Jacob, who wrestled the angel, we now walk with a limp. We may lose a hand or our sight, have our heart broken or our house burn to the ground. But somewhere in the midst of this confrontation, we are transformed.

We see this in life of the Christian killer, Saul, who meets Christ, is blinded temporarily, and then becomes Paul. Abram leaves everything and becomes Abraham. Jacob the "heel grabber" becomes Israel, who "wrestles with God." Simon becomes Peter, "the Rock." We see a transformation in the scarred and risen Christ.

After Golgotha, he returns similar but *changed*. He is harder to recognize and less restricted by the laws of earth. Soon, we will see him as the Coming King, revealed and riding his white horse.

Spiritually, we are transformed when we confront ourselves and our mortality, surrendering our lives at the feet of the Living One. We receive gifts, calling, and are endowed with supernatural power and wisdom for the journey.

When it happens, we are not fully aware of our transformation.

Something feels different, but our change is usually more noticeable to others. We walk without fear, with purpose and intention. Our brow is creased and our eyes are narrowed as we prowl through life. Others are uncomfortable by our wildness, by our pulsing and dangerous courage. When we face the bear, we take something from him. Or rather, he offers it to us with a glance.

At home, people no longer take advantage of us. We no longer avoid eye contact, lowering ourselves beneath others. We lift our head, fix our gaze, and straighten our shoulders.

The transformed man no longer walks in shame or fear.

When the trials come, we do not submit to them, or accept them as impending defeat. We do not roll over. We now face our boss or our employees or the person who wishes to encroach on us with equal courage; we no longer shy away from the heat of conflict. We are changed.

After our confrontation and transformation, we **return** to the village.

We come back as black knights or bearded warriors. Saint Augustine talks about this bearded man: "The beard signifies the courageous...the earnest, the active, the vigorous. So that when we describe such [a man], we say, he is a bearded man."[6]

Right now I'm thinking of a boy named Max.

In *Where the Wild Things Are*, Max was taken away from the bedroom of his mother's house, sailing east on a great red boat. Crashing through the rising waters, over thundertops and jagged crops, he sailed. Over dawns and dusks and through pelting rain and pounding waves. Chill winds moaned and bit at him, stinging his cheeks.

Gone for weeks and weeks and then a year, Max lost everything and everyone he once knew. He crashed upon the rocks and climbed out. Wandered into the forest looking and calling for help. But no one responded. No one heard.

Soon Max was lost.

After his initial shock and grief, Max somehow managed to control his fear. Until suddenly he came face-to-face with the Wild Things. Maurice Sendak describes them, "Roaring their terrible roars, gnashing their terrible teeth, rolling their terrible eyes, and showing their terrible claws."

The Wild Things were huge, looming beasts. Terrible.

But Max learned to defeat them with a simple magic trick: He stared at their yellow eyes without blinking. Once Max summoned the courage to confront them, he won, and became *King of the Wild Things!*[7]

Our story is not Max's story, but there are similarities. Max leaves Mom. After a "terrible" confrontation, he masters his fear and wins. In some ways, Max is changed. But he comes back to his mother's pillow the same little boy, not as *King of the Wild Things!*

In the woods we find new life and, like Max, become: *King of the Wild Things!* But we return home the same as before. Internally, we are different. Externally, we are still Max—the son of our mother. Even though we conquered the terrible Wild Things, no one at home sees us as the *Wild King.*

Culture pushes back against us. It fears and resists the *Bearded Man.* It mocks the man with edges, the man with his own opinions, and the outspoken man. The man who stands against the *vox populi* is greeted with ridicule and scorn. Before long, we doubt if we ever were the *Wild Kings* at all.

Some men never return home.

Today's man is crippled by Something Awful, by fear, confusion, fatherless pain, and inadequacy. Culture steers him away from the woods. He faces a challenge but stops short of claiming his true identity.

Like Max, he is stuck in his mom's house, mired in adultlescence. Or he never comes back, stuck on the swirling islands of Perelandra.

The village does not know it *needs* the wild masculine. It needs:

Wild Kings. Bearded Men. Weight-Bearing Men. Dangerous Men.

The village needs men who head into the woods and kill whatever is eating the livestock. It needs men who can charge remote beaches, men who can fight, not just at work, but also at home.

The world needs Living Myth now more than ever.

It needs men like my friend CJ, who moved from California to the projects of Portland to live among the needy, the poor, and thousands of homeless teenagers—to restore dignity and love them quietly and without fanfare.

CJ is talented; he is smart and strong. He started roasting Tanager Coffee, and in a few months, he was winning awards. CJ looks like the lead singer of Imagine Dragons, and when he chops wood, it splits into four pieces. He could do anything he wants, but he is there, fixing bikes for homeless people, feeding them meals, fighting for them. And he refuses to use the word "homeless," instead saying, "people who live outside."

CJ is a *Bearded Man.*

The world needs my friend Cameron, who builds stuff. He is a master builder, making decks, reclaimed furniture, concrete bars, and coffee shops. He built an epic recording studio for our friend Josh.

Cameron is a tireless servant, and he has a white German shepherd who follows him around lock-step. Cameron goes into the hardware store, makes her sit outside, and when he comes out an hour later, she hasn't moved. I love that dog.

Whenever it would rain, the basement of my Portland house liked to flood. This means it flooded for nine months. Cameron fixed it. Months later, it was starting to flood again, and before I could call him, he was at my house, setting up a pump inside and on his knees outside, bucketing out water in the rain and the mud. Cameron worked for hours, at six o'clock in the morning on a Sunday. This is what he does. He is a tireless servant to his friends, his neighbors, and his wife.

Cameron is a *Bearded Man*.

It is easier for us never to return. Or to hide our beards if we do return. It is easier to stay in California making bank. Or to hit the "ignore" button on our phone when we get that early morning call. We may allow ourselves to be subdued or silenced, pretending, like Peter, we've never met the *Bearded Man*.

It takes courage to stand up to the hostile village.

It takes courage to *claim your mythic ground*.

The return means giving our whole lives, bringing vitality and wildness to the community. *Bearded Men* of yesteryear returned from the woods to build cities and orphanages, hospitals, and churches. These men saw the unseen and lived for the "now and not yet." They joined the ranks of those who build the invisible kingdom.

These are our mythic steps.

Severance. Confrontation. Transformation. Return.

My late-night conversation with Lewis and Tolkien gave me hope. It lit a torch and showed me a path. What if the mythic rhythms, uncovered by generations of storytellers, were actually beacons and signs? I brushed up against these rhythms on Kodiak—now a road was rising up to meet me.

The mythic steps point us to the ancient man secrets. They point us to the True Myth. Like the mythic heroes before him, Christ followed a distinct route, a heroic path. His initiation moved him from his mother's house away into the river, then to the wilderness and into manhood. Riding a donkey, he returned to the village as King. He faced his mortality at Golgotha and, after three days, conquered death.

These steps are divinely ordained for Christ's movement into manhood. And they are divinely ordained for us. These mythic steps are our initiation; they steer us to the ManCave, to the true harbor.

CHAPTER SEVEN

Movimentio Es Vida

To start our mythic journey, we must be severed
from the world, from the popular voice, and
from even ourselves.

Every journey begins with a step. It is a step away, a *severance*. It begins with leaving home, with movement. Reluctance is normal; we are stationary creatures. It's hard to say what compels us forward. A moment of inspiration, or spiritual awakening. The death of a friend, loss of a job or a relationship. Stepping on the scales and realizing we've let ourselves go. Dissatisfaction. Disruption. Or a magnificent defeat.

Life has not turned out as planned.

When everything to lose has been lost and we are at the end of all things, we may then find the recklessness to take the first step. When Thoreau's "quiet desperation" becomes a deafening roar, we may pay attention. Whatever force drives us forward, we only change when we embrace fear and walk through the Dark Door.

Tim Ferriss calls this awakening the "Harajuku Moment."[1] He insists no change happens without it. No matter how well organized we are. Our best-laid plans, our New Year's wishes, and P90X workout videos all fall flat unless the "nice to have" becomes the "must have."

My Harajuku Moment happened the night my girls were born.

When I held them, my fear was eclipsed by love. Whatever life threw at me, I would *handle it* for the sake of my girls. I didn't know everything, or the "right way" to be a dad, but I was bound and determined to figure it out.

In the months after they were born, I worked hard to give them what they needed. My friend Jon Collins told me to be the "best husband I could be," as my wife would be doing the lion's share. So I stayed up late nights and changed as many diapers as possible. I learned the bathtub songs. I took them to the park and gave Kari some breaks. I gave them all as much love and affection as possible.

My questions about fatherhood shined a light on broader issues—the questions I still had about being a man and a husband. I felt incomplete. I felt uncertain, stuck in the mud, but I couldn't say why.

Something Awful was closer than ever before.

I gained 40 pounds, which was reflective of how I felt. I had spent years writing and thinking and talking about rejection and fatherlessness. I felt like it was my banner, my calling to activate the church to reach the fatherless generation. Speaking and living so close to the grief took its toll.

The calling felt personal, which made it hard to have healthy boundaries. So I wrote and spoke and traveled and worked myself into the ground, believing if I could just get more mentors, more young lives would be changed. This led to wildly unrealistic expectations and ended in disappointment. I always felt like I wasn't doing enough, there had to be more.

I needed to work on my marriage. I traveled constantly, speaking and training mentors, sometimes gone from home two weeks at a time. It is hard to sustain a relationship when one spouse lives on the road. My wife was a trooper but we needed to reconnect. The travel was for a season; now I needed to be a moss gatherer.

During that season, I grew more and more dissatisfied.

My body started breaking down. I ground my teeth and had

cold sweats at night. After one particular mentor training, I watched the video of me teaching. I sounded tired and flat. I was overweight, haggard, and worn out.

Something *had* to change.

These are tipping points. Opportunities for seismic paradigm shifts. Our normal routine has been disrupted, and our long-held assumptions are challenged. Whatever life we have settled for, we now see the cold, hard truth.

We are not who we were born to be.

Some seize the moment and change. Many men accept less and settle.

Most never take the first step. "Things are not that bad," we think. So we reach for another Twinkie. We go on floating, living in gelatinous complacency. We play it safe, staying far away from the lonely mountain.

We seek adventure with our remote control, tuning in to find action on the gridiron, or by watching *Walking Dead*. Severance exists as a fantasy in our minds, during a pickup truck commercial, or playing a video game. We are entertained but bored. We seem to have everything we need: two cars, a mortgage, clothes, the newest technology, and a 401(k), but life feels flat.

The coho stirring is alive deep within us.

We dream about being extraordinary, about living with action and danger, but make no significant intention in that direction. It's hard to pinpoint what went wrong along the way. Bankruptcy. Our house got repossessed. Our marriage skidded to a stalemate. Our youthful, idealistic edge was dulled by repeated failures.

For this man, movement feels impossible.

He sinks down into discontented acceptance of a less-than life. Sits in his self-imposed cage of victimization and grief. Coasts from job to vacation to relationship with no other intention than to arrive safely at death. He has vivid dreams about moving away from the madness, facing the chaos and winning the fight.

This is the fantasy of the Doomsday Prepper Movement.

Preppers are training and gearing up for the postapocalyptic world.

My friend Dave collects watches; I collect Bug Out Bags. The BOB is the icon of the Prepper Movement. He tells me about his Explorers, Omegas, and U Boat Flightdeck watches. I tell him about water purifiers, wool socks, machetes, and multi-tools.

He says the big-faced watches, the ones over 42mm, are trendy and will go the way of all trends. He prefers the Omegas, which Buzz Aldrin wore on the moon. He likes them not for the show, or for impressing his hoity-toity friends, but for the right reasons—the craftsmanship, the excellence, the stories they tell.

He can have his watches; I'll keep my zombie gear.

The basic premise of the movement is this: The zombies (or something worse) are coming soon. Society is fragile and unraveling fast. The Preppers live while the unprepared become walking corpses. Millions of aspiring zombie hunters, anarchists, and survivalists have become Preppers.

The Bug Out Bag is your first line of defense.

You grab it when you see your neighbor trying to bite your dog. Or when the Yoga Mom at Whole Foods eats red meat straight from the package.

Something is *definitely* wrong.

These are signs of the end. But since no one knows when the zombies are coming, Doomsday Preppers must be ready for anything. Nuclear fallout. Locusts. Economic collapse. Viral pandemic. Civil war.

To help you better understand Prepper subculture—which features dozens of creative acronyms—I've compiled a short list of basic terminology:

BOB—Bug Out Bag (the Prepper icon, usually a backpack)

BOV—Bug Out Vehicle

BOL—Bug Out Location

BIL—Bug In Location

SHTF—Stuff Hits the Fan

EMP—Electro-Magnetic Pulse (a weapon that knocks out electronics)

GOOD—Get Out of Dodge

OTG—Off the Grid

MRE—Meal Ready to Eat

WROL—Without Rule of Law

TEOTWAWKI—The End of the World as We Know It

The idea is this: When the SHTF and zombies or locusts or whatever comes, you grab your BOB and burn rubber out of town. The contents of your BOB are a huge point of contention for Preppers. *New York Times* best-selling books debate the perfect ingredients. I think it depends on your geography and purpose. You could have several different BOBs. One for the hospital delivery room. One is weather-centric, for tornadoes or hurricanes. And one, of course, for the zombie horde.

There are lots of pretenders and wannabes out there.

Yesterday, I walked into a small "Prepper" store—somewhere west of the Rockies. I envisioned meeting guys who were dressed in urban digital camo, wearing machetes and gas masks. You know, the hard-core, off-the-grid, *Book of Eli* types. They'd have a rack of vintage weapons, and hidden behind that rack, they'd have the good stuff, like RPGs, flamethrowers, and a secret, underground bunker.

When I got inside, the place was clean and swept. No guns. No knives. It did have a cool ghillie suit. It also had cheap trinkets, kitschy-touristy stuff, such as Luchador masks, belt buckles with hidden knives, and posters of Sarah Conner and Mad Max.

Behind the counter stood a young guy, probably nineteen, who looked too kind to be a Prepper. He was clean and had a sunny deposition.

"Hey there, bud," he offered in a high-pitched voice.

"Do you guys sell Bug Out Bags?" I asked.

It was more quiz than question.

"No, but we can make 'em," he said in his pleasant, singsongy tone.

Not a bad answer, I thought. "So do you recommend the K-Bar or Gerber machete? Serrated edge or no?"

I was probing, testing his mettle.

"I don't know much about machetes, but we do have a keychain pocketknife."

A key-chain pocketknife—*seriously?*

He lost serious street cred.

I hoped the tourist vibe was just a front, a ruse to keep away guys looking for a photo op. Maybe I needed the secret code or needed to pass some unwritten test to see the good stuff and meet the Prepper Guru.

I threw out a couple Prepper acronyms. Talked about the ongoing wars in the Middle East, the vanishing honeybees, disturbing weather trends, economic collapse, and viral pandemics. I asked him a question about Glocks. But he had never heard of a Glock.

Instead, he tried to sell me a pink rabbit's foot—*a rabbit's foot*. "We also have these in lime green," he added.

"What?" I wanted to shout.

"What are you even saying to me right now? A rabbit's foot? Do you think zombies like their ears tickled? Do you think TEO-TWAWKI is a joke? What do you think this is—*Comic-Con?*"

This was a tourist shop. I was wasting my time. While I was shopping for rabbit's feet, true Preppers were out there somewhere, gearing up and getting ready for Z. It takes more than a store title to be a zombie hunter.

Moving on.

I think a good zombie BOB contains: Printed map to your BOL—with four alternative routes, as GPS may be down. Pocket water purifier. Nalgene bottles and/or CamelBak insert. Dozen MREs. Compass. First-aid kit. Weatherproof lighter. Firestarter. Pistol or rifle with extra clips. (Much debate here over brand/caliber. I like the Remington 870 shotgun.) Sleeping bag. Tarp. Hatchet or Cold Steel Machete. Roll of paracord. Multi-tool. (I prefer Leatherman, hand-made in Portland.) There are ten thousand good options.

Here are a few custom items most Preppers miss: Sunscreen. A sky without an ozone layer will fry you or damage your retinas. Tinted goggles, same reason. Gas mask, as there is likely to be a ton of ashes, pollution, and zombie dust in the air. Do you really want to breathe all that? Gold or silver coins, for bartering. Fishing gear and/or small game traps. Remember: Your BOB is only packed for a 72-hour emergency scenario, not intended for long-term sustainability. It is for the flight stage, for the GOOD, and for leaving the urban sprawl.

Once you have your BOB packed with the right gear—sans rabbit foot—you are ready to load up your BOV. Preferably, your BOV is an older, diesel engine, four-wheel-drive vehicle. The lack of electronics makes it EMP resistant. If you're alone, a dirt-bike motocross is a good option. Whatever you have, whether bicycle or boots, get moving. As Brad Pitt rightly says in *World War Z,* "*Movimentio es vida.*"[2]

Movement is life.

With BOB in hand, you get moving, heading out on your pre-arranged route to your BOL. Your BOL is at least one fuel tank away from a major city; it is OTG and stocked with the rest of your gear, sustainable for long-term living.

Think: Low pop. Deep woods or vacant mountains. Low visibility, unable to be seen from a road or the air. Water source(s). Security. Heirloom vegetables and legumes. Weather resistant, able to withstand the four seasons.

The Prepper scenario is all about leaving home.

It is driven by many things, including the desire for survival, to "always be prepared" and ready for whatever may come. On the negative side, it is fueled by fear and worry, changing world events and terrorism, and an overactive imagination. We fantasize about it, spending billions of dollars watching TV shows and movies about it. But we don't know how to get our arms around it. Much of the Prepper appeal comes from our strong desire for *severance.*

Some buy into a false idea of severance.

We learned this by watching our fathers leave. Life is always greener, so we become perpetual fence-hoppers. We leave home, jump ship, and abandon family.

Culture also gives us an escape route.

It tells us we can "fall in and out of love," like a pit. This absolves us of any and all responsibility. "Hey, I know I have children, responsibility, and people count on me, but I'm leaving. It's not my fault, I'm just not in love anymore."

This man leaves his wife and children, has a midlife crisis. He dumps the weight, moves to a distant city, and sets up another franchise family.

This man feels the mythic stirring, but moves in the wrong direction.

We learn false severance by watching corporate greed tank the global economy. We see "The Man" fire us and hundreds of our hardworking friends. If "The Man" isn't loyal to us, why should we be loyal to him or anyone else? So we turn our backs on him, changing jobs in the time it takes to post a new Craigslist ad.

We know how to depart, but not with intentional direction. Our leaving has no goal, no destination in mind. We are rootless, feeling like postapocalyptic floaters. Wraiths haunting the ruins of our father's landscape, we scavenge for scraps amid the ruins. Like Francis Schaeffer said, we are men with "both feet firmly planted in mid-air."

Our heart longs for the woods, but we're stuck, paralyzed by fear. We're too content, too complacent, and too afraid to leave home.

When Cus D'Amato trained a champion, his first lesson was about fear. He knew fear would paralyze the most talented fighter. So he taught men to embrace fear, to recognize and use it against their enemies.

Cus used the example of a deer, who detects a mountain lion nearby. Normally the deer could jump ten or so feet, but with the fear, he runs faster and jumps twenty feet. The fear activates something powerful in him, something that protects him, and even saves his life. Fear is nature's way to prepare us for struggle.

Mike Tyson recalled Cus saying, "The hero and the coward both feel the same thing, but the hero uses his fear, projects it onto his opponent, while the coward runs. *It's the same thing, fear, but it's what you do with it that matters.*"[3]

The man who avoids fear misses life.

He is afraid of ridicule, afraid of looking foolish, afraid of pain. Afraid of the *vox populi*, or of Something Awful. As long as he stays in the safety of the village, he may be able to avoid fear altogether, other than the fear that holds him still. But he will never have a Harajuku Moment.

Marine Stephen Pressfield writes, "Being paralyzed with fear is a good sign. Like self-doubt, fear is an indicator. Fear tells us what we have to do. The more scared we are of a calling, the more sure we can be that we have to do it."[4]

In the face of fear—*movimentio es vida.*

Our first step is shaky. The road to the Skull is treacherous. It's covered in ash, littered with debris and burned-out vehicles. The road signs are burned or lying in the ditch. There are endless detours and cul-de-sacs.

When we do reach the woods, they are strangely bent and twisted. We are surrounded by reaching trees, creaking and swiping. We see bones strewn across the path. We hear gurgling noises, shuffling, and strange growls. Vultures loom overhead.

The woods feels like a sweltering, breathing place, a hungry, living thing waiting to swallow us whole.

Many men flee the woods. But we do have another option.

We can close our eyes. Slow down our breathing. Get still and let the danger heighten our senses. Our heartbeat soon matches the breath of the living trees. In the words of Eden Phillpotts, "The world is full of magic things, patiently waiting for our senses to grow sharper."[5]

In the woods, our senses do grow sharper. Our pupils widen and adjust to the pale moonlight. We make our own path, prowling through the limbs, careful not to step on twigs or dry leaves. We come across faint traces of elfish magic on the air, invisible threads to follow. Sometimes, the magic finds us.

If we listen close enough, somewhere off in the distance, the mythic rhythm howls, long and wolfish. This is our call. Like Buck from *The Call of the Wild*,[6] the song of our ancestors runs deep in us. And when we heed it, we discover the primal within. But the only way to hear it again is to point our nose at a star and *howl back*.

Movement changes us.

Movement in one area can translate into widespread movement. Some decisions give us willpower and courage to face the other. These decisions ripple across our psyche like flat stones across the pond.

Sometimes all it takes is one choice. One defiance of normalcy. One attack against a bad habit. One rebellion against complacency. The choice acts as a wedge, breaking in, moving, creating momentum.

Then momentum becomes an avalanche.

New York Times reporter Charles Duhigg calls this a "keystone habit."[7] This is the one decision that generates momentum in other areas of our lives. We don't have to change everything at once; we just need to change one habit. Moving in the right direction is success. Success, even the smallest success, creates momentum and confidence. Courage begets courage. It's brick and mortar.

Even though it is small, it's something.

This is what I did. Bob was right—I could be homeland security.

I knew I could *do* that.

I could protect my daughters. I might suck at singing sleepy songs or learning how to comb hair. (I haven't owned a comb or brush since high school.) I might not know how to sew or change a diaper or hold a baby right, but I can shoot somebody in the face with a bottle rocket.

Movement changes us.

We're no longer sitting down, no longer stationary creatures. We are no longer reactionaries or passive victims of circumstance. We're now walking tall, facing and moving forward. We lean into life and create new opportunities. We move from watcher to walker, from hoarder to explorer, and from victim to hunter. This shift changes us and stirs the eternal. In his 1951 book *The Scottish Himalayan Expedition*, W. H. Murray writes:

Until one is committed, there is hesitancy, the chance to draw back. Concerning all acts of initiative and creation, there is one elementary truth: the moment you definitely commit yourself, then Providence moves too. All sorts of things occur that would never otherwise have occurred. A whole stream of events issue from that one decision, raising all manner of unforeseen incidents and meetings and material assistance, which no man could have dreamed would come his way. *Whatever you can do, or dream you can do, begin it. Boldness has genius, power, and magic in it. Begin it now.*[8]

CHAPTER EIGHT

Into the Red Earth

To move forward, we need to let go of bitterness
and the victim story. We must forgive our
fathers.

A few years ago, I started hunting dinosaurs with my friend Reggie. In his office, he has a full-bodied Allo-saurus, which is a smaller version of T. rex. He also has Triceratops, Spinosaurus, and T. rex skulls. He has tons of other fossils: Megalodon teeth, bones, eggs, and hooked claws. He calls his office "Indiana Jones's Garage."

At Reggie's invitation, we drove out to "No Man's Land"—the name given to unincorporated America. It was the place people went to be forgotten. It was the Robbers Roost—housing crooks, gold stealers, moonshine dealers, criminals, and out-laws. We were an hour away from "civilization," which was a one-stoplight town. No cell phone. No electricity. The first night someone nearly stepped on a rattlesnake, and the winds howled and gusted so hard they snapped the poles of our tents.

No Man's Land, quite a place.

We arrived at the dig site the next morning. Reggie's crew had uncovered part of a massive vertebra, about the size of my waist. It was buried deep under granite and clay. I helped my friend Boone pull some brown rib fossils out of the ground. Later, I held a full *mastodon* thighbone. I couldn't get my head around it. Big hairy elephants walked around New Mexico, Oklahoma, and Colorado? Wild.

The dig was not what I'd expected.

It wasn't dramatic, like *Raiders of the Lost Ark*. With Egyptian workers digging and singing Arabic songs on the hill, as the gray thunder and Nazis close in. Rather, it was slow, methodic, and measured. The rock quarry was squared off by tape, cataloged, and numbered. The tiniest fragment was treasured and mapped.

When you unearth fossils, you don't relentlessly hammer the ground, as if digging for water. After getting through the limestone and into the clay, you use the small tools. You whittle. You brush. You scoop out cups of dirt. It may take two hours to fill a small bucket with dirt. It may take weeks to go through a foot of clay. Most of the actual "digging" takes place with ice picks and small paintbrushes.

Something happens to me when I dig.

I'm filled with anticipation. Finding new things, arrowheads and flint-hewn knives. Rib fragments and teeth. As every inch is painstakingly uncovered, I am filled with expectation. I sense my impatience, and learn that hurry ruins everything. It takes heaps of patient determination to keep digging, to go farther down and farther in.

Severance is our move forward, but also downward. It is patiently getting under the limestone and into the red earth. Mythic severance is often a move below, beneath what is seen. It is *subterranean*.

Downward is the first direction for a lot of us.

This is an inner severance. This is having the courage to grieve, or wake up. It is facing the yellow eyes, facing our despair or guilt, our rejection or loss. It may or may not be connected to our lost fathers. Some simply lost their appetite for dreaming. Dreams have been replaced by a mixture of depression and cynicism. Our dreams have died. We have become Langston Hughes's "broken-winged bird"; our life is now "a barren field, frozen over with snow."

We need to look inward, accept our loses, and admit that something has died. Others need to run at breakneck speed toward life. It may be high time to climb the lonely mountain, stand on our hind paws, and roar like a Barbary lion. Others need to sit in the ashes and grieve.

My parents divorced when I was two.

Dad moved to Austin, and we saw him once or twice a year. I remember his early visits, when he drove up from Austin to Little Rock for the weekend. I was around four or five; things seemed good. The wintry effects of divorce had not yet reached its chill fingers into my soul. In the words of Bly, I had not yet lost my "golden ball."

My brother took Polaroid pictures of us at the park. I remember the swings, trying to swing as high as him, trying to make him proud. I have a picture sitting on Dad's lap in front of the Christmas tree. I was five, grinning and wearing a brown bomber jacket, one of those with a white, furry collar. We had just opened Christmas presents and I was holding a board game with an ironic name—*Sorry!*

Shortly after taking that picture, Dad drove back to Austin.

I remember watching him drive away. My little family fantasy was incinerated—burned to ashes. I cried uncontrollably, convulsing. I staggered into the living room, plopped down on the plaid couch, and cried. No amount of crying, no comfort from my mother, could ever bring him back. He was gone.

That was the moment I lost my golden ball.

Over the next few years, I reimagined life without him. My mom and grandmother faithfully loved and raised me. But there were no men around. I grew suspicious, and had deep insecurities about being a man. The unspoken assumption was, "If dad doesn't care to be around, how could anyone else?"

I felt stranded at the bottom of Fireman's Hill.

Whenever it snowed, neighborhood kids hiked over to the Fire Station and rode sleds down the Hill. Sleds were trash can lids, cardboard boxes, pieces of aluminum siding, anything we could find. Our moms warned us to be careful, to watch out for cars. Mom told me about the poor kid who slid under a parked car and broke his neck.

Once we slid to the bottom, we took the long hike back for another run.

I began to see the world like this.

Everyone else was at the top of the hill, while I stood alone at the bottom. And it was a long, hard climb to get back up. The world shifted; it was no longer a level playing field. It made me feel fragile. Insecure. I know I'm not alone in this. Anger or shame fill the void left by an absent father.

My friend Shaun Alexander also has this story. He told me:

I grew up in a single-parent home with my mom and my brother. Dad had nine kids with four different women. You don't want to tell your story because you feel like less of a person. And you don't want to go through the war of what people think about you. It was only after years playing at Alabama, after my years with the Seattle Seahawks, that I began to realize there is a success story in the midst of my mental war.

We may break the NFL single-season record for touchdowns. Or have millions of people cheering for us every Sunday, or win the MVP. But if we grew up in a fatherless hut, we can live in shame and feel like less of a person.

I mentored a young boy when we lived in Los Angeles. After we had hung out for a year or so, I asked if he ever saw his dad. "I don't have a dad," he replied innocently, without guile. This was just his reality. Then he asked, *"Will you be my dad?"*

This is a question a lot of men still ask.

I still asked it well into my twenties.

We want Dad's approval; we want him to be proud. If Dad is dead or gone, we may still look for approval from his ghost. I hated my insecurity and was ashamed of it. It wasn't until years later I was forced to confront it. I left a job where my boss was a father figure.

Later, I realized many bosses were my surrogate father figures. I moved from job to job looking for the perfect boss-dad. Each boss-dad became an unsuspecting victim of my impossible expectations. These relationships ended predictably, in disappointment.

This particular boss-dad had no idea. Poor guy. I mean, he knew I looked up to him. But I never came out and asked him to be my dad. I never gave him a "dad contract" or asked to take a blood oath with him or anything. I left the job under good terms. It was my choice, actually.

Nothing crazy happened. Some minor tension, but nothing juicy to write about. I didn't steal a church pew. I didn't kill anybody's cat with a potato gun. I just knew I wasn't supposed to be there anymore and it was time to leave.

But on my way out, our relationship changed. As I look back, it felt like cold professionalism, way less personal than my lofty dad-expectation demanded.

It felt like rejection. It wasn't. It was rejection of my false hope, for sure. Just another boss-dad who left me sitting alone at the Christmas tree. Looking back, it was all so weird. Why I even cared so much in the first place. I guess when you secretly ask guys to be your dad, you wind up disappointed. And I've talked to a lot of other men who do the same thing.

After leaving the job, I was in pain. Even though my boss-dad marriage proposals were as realistic as flying opossums. I felt too much pain, not an appropriate amount for the situation. I remember crying afterward. I mean, I'm a pretty sensitive guy, but I'm not a huge crier. What was going on? Why on earth was I crying?

I got alone, prayed, and asked God for help. For anything.

It felt like I heard his answer almost immediately.

—You are mourning the loss of your father—

The loss of my latest boss-dad triggered a bigger grief. For all of my life, I pursued boss-dads because I still desperately wanted one. My response to this emerging pain was critical. I could have ignored it, and resumed my hunt for boss-dads. I could have hidden and stuffed it away like before. Or dismissed it, saying it was psychobabble, and despised it, giving birth to more shame.

The best thing I did was to admit it mattered.

The next few months were huge.

I met with Gail, who my friends call "The Oracle."

Gail gave me sage advice. Advice, according to Gildor the Elf, "is a dangerous gift, even from the wise to the wise."[1] This is especially true during times of grief or vulnerability. Everyone is willing to speak into our lives. People mean well, with their religious platitudes and self-help clichés, but a lot of them aren't helpful at all.

Getting wisdom is key. Bad advice is like visiting a shady chiropractor. We leave his office with a throbbing back, worse off than when we walked in. The Oracle told me, "Remember those early moments, try to think of those early images. The images in your head when your father left. Get alone. Think about them, and mourn them."

So I did. I spent about an hour a day praying and writing.

Then I would close the journal.

Closing the journal was a signal for me to go and live. I think it's easy to get consumed in grief, and then spend long days, even months and years, sitting in the ashes. Sometimes the grief becomes our identity. Journaling was a way to open my soul to God. To reflect, mourn, pray. When I finished for the day, I gave myself permission to go live, and come back again tomorrow.

During that time of reflection, the best thing I did was to get alone, and open my heart to the One who is "a man of sorrows, familiar with suffering" (Isaiah 53:3). Jesus alone has traveled the far islands of grief and loneliness. "A bruised reed he will not break, a smoldering wick he will not snuff out" (Isaiah 42:3).

It wasn't religious or ritualistic. It was more about falling into him. There was no pressure to perform. It felt like that Mute Math song in which they sing, "*It's okay, it's okay,*" over and over again.[2] Thomas Merton put it this way:

> Surrender. Whether you understand it or not, God loves you, is present in you, lives in you, calls you, saves you and offers you an understanding and compassion which are like nothing you have ever found in a book or heard in a sermon.[3]

I stopped dancing, stopped hiding. Held out my heart with upward-facing palms. When I did, something changed. Something shifted. I was finding place. More than anything else, God wants to restore our *place*. He wants us to stop dancing, hiding, performing, running. He wants to reclaim us as sons and daughters. And all he asks is that we respond to his divine overture.

As I drained the cup of grief, life slowed down.

Men are told not to cry; tears are a sign of weakness. I grew up afraid of my shame; I hated how fragile it made me. As I wept, I found the opposite to be true. It took courage for me to sit down in the ash heap and mourn. The grief was not making me weaker—it was setting me free. Martin Shaw adds:

"Wildness is the capacity to go into joy, sorrow, and anger fully and stay there as long as needed, regardless of what anyone else thinks. Wildness carries sobriety as well as exuberance, and has allowed loss to mark its face."[4]

Even the Wolf King is not afraid to mourn.

After months of journaling, praying, digging, and staying in the grief, something felt different. I was still aware of the pain, but the tears were gone. The wound was no longer open. It was cauterized.

So I went to talk to The Oracle again. This time, she said I had fully grieved the pain. It was time to close and seal the journal. I did.

Then I called my dad.

Our conversation went something like this: "You know you need to come to Austin to see your grandma. She might die soon. You really need to come down here."

"Yes, Dad, I know."

My grandma lived in a nursing home in Austin. At the time, she didn't have any life-threatening medical problems or complications. Dad was right, I did need to see her and my grandpa. I remember those few times, as a child, when Grandpa took me fishing. He taught me how to play five-card draw and Texas hold'em. Each time I went to Austin, he measured my height with a pencil on the pantry door.

For some reason, I got upset. Past conversations always stayed in the veneer of college football or baseball or patriotism. Safe spaces. We never talked about relationships or conflict. But something clicked in me and I spoke up.

"Dad, you left. You're the one who drove off and left. So you can't give me a guilt trip now that I'm not around."

Silence.

It came out harsh, but I wasn't trying to be harsh. I wasn't lashing out; I just said it. And when I did, I realized I'd crossed into uncharted territory. So I kept going. I told him about the time he drove off, leaving me sitting there by the Christmas tree holding the *Sorry!* game. I told him how I was shattered, and how, eventually, I stopped hoping altogether.

His response surprised me:

"I cried, too. Every time I got back in the car and drove away."

And he was crying right then, on the phone.

This was new. There was something inside my dad that cared. His grief didn't fix everything on the spot. But it was new. I knew he cared and liked me, but always assumed his leaving was heartless and cold and unfeeling. For years, demons convinced me of his indifference. Sometimes no demons are needed—as distance and lack of interest are pretty convincing, too.

When he wept, I saw he was not a dark cyborg after all, but a human. His crying didn't mean everything was hunky-dory. Nor did it mean he would instantly transform into the Perfect Dad, a bald, white, bearded version of Bill Cosby.

But it was a start. It was something. And it changed my perspective.

A few years later, he asked me to officiate his father's funeral. I didn't know my grandpa well, which was my biggest grief. I went to see him right before he died. Told him I was sorry I didn't get to know him better, and thanked him for the few times he took me fishing. I thanked him for teaching me how to play poker. I told him if we'd lived closer, we probably would've been great pals. He smiled.

His funeral was small. It was only my dad's extended family. No priests or pastors. Just me and Chris, two grandsons who lived in different cities. Chris played the guitar. I talked about the grandfather I wished I knew better. The grandfather I wanted to see and fish with again.

A couple years later, I didn't tell Dad I wrote *Fatherless Generation*.

It was a coward move. In my defense, I didn't want to deal with any drama. And I honestly didn't think he would read it or hear about it. I tried to honor him in the writing, while staying true to my own story.

The reality is I saw him once or twice a year, and heard from him about the same. I liked seeing him, and was grateful that he never went off the grid, like other dads. But it wasn't until later, in my mid-twenties, that I realized how hard this was. Close friends told me I couldn't describe the fatherless generation and leave my story out. I wasn't writing it as an accusation or a guilt trip but as an honest expression of what I felt.

After it was published, I planned to tell him about it. He found out about the book before I had the chance. I'm sure it wounded him. Even worse, there was no conclusion. I wrote about my rejection and shame. I wrote about the pain I felt and how I lived for his ghost. But my storyline disappeared. I left it open-ended and unresolved.

There was no tidy or redemptive ending. Maybe there wasn't any resolution in my heart yet. The loudest part of my story was grief. Grief was my expression and my calling, to sit in the sooty ashes with a rejected generation.

After writing the book, I felt like my story still needed a resolution. It needed a conclusion. There was no return from the grief forest. Maybe the return trip is more difficult than I realized.

We must forgive our fathers.

Dad may have passed away. Or be locked up. Maybe we never knew him. Whatever the case, we need to make peace. We need to let go of bitterness and the victim story. We will never move forward if we don't, never become the men we were born to be. Someone once said, "The man who curses his father curses his destiny."

Before we set out for the deep woods in search of the wild masculine, some need to mourn. The loss of our father. The loss of our mother. The pain of divorce, abuse, loss. As children, it's natural for us to forget, repress, and lock away the grief and pain. It's our defense mechanism. Sometimes we never unlock it.

Men have a capacity to forget, to compartmentalize. We

store pain for years in a buried, rusty toolbox. We push through and pretend it doesn't matter. We gash a bloody hole in our left calf with a handsaw, rub some dirt on it, and keep going. We think, "It's not that big of a deal." Some of us do this our whole lives.

Keep going.

We push ahead, even when our entrails drag along the ground.

It takes man-sized courage to stop, to look down at our wound and admit it mattered. Until we do that, we will never experience our full life, love, or emotion. We live slumped over, under the weight of fear and shame. We are afraid of the grief forest, and afraid, too, of the sunrise and the joyous ocean breakers. We're afraid of disapproval from our peers, our girlfriend or wife, or our current boss-dad.

It takes courage to stop and dig our fingers into the red earth. When we find the courage to be honest, to grieve, to forgive and release, we find freedom. And as a new father, I pray my children will extend me the same grace. I love them deeply, but know I have cracks and flaws.

I look forward to going on more trips with my dad. Maybe one day we will go to Australia and swim with the great whites. Or jump around with the Maasai. Or go to the Amazon to spear-hunt jaguars, like Sasha Siemel. When I got home from Alaska, I sent him this e-mail:

Thank you for the Kodiak trip. I've hunted my whole life, chased deer and boars and ducks. But hunting Kodiak was a bigger thrill, more intense and thrilling than any of those. There is something eerie about being a few steps away from a bear, as it stares at you and crunches bones. I'm really grateful for our time together. It was great being with you and Chris, and it's something I will always remember. If you are up for it, I'd love to go on more adventures with you.

CHAPTER NINE

The River

Our leaving home is supernatural. It is Spirit-led.

Severance is a beginning, a genesis. It requires a step. Then another. It is a movement forward, but it's also a movement *away*. It is a move away from the familiar places, the ruts and well-hiked trails. Before it can be a new beginning, it is an *ending*.

The Brothers Grimm are partly right. They suggest our first step toward the wild masculine is stealing the key from Mom. After all, the key to *Hairy Man*'s cage rests safely under her pillow. We must steal the key to let him out.

Severance does mean stepping away from Mom, stepping away from the world and every other horizontal voice. But it's more than a reaction to Mom. It is not Mom-centric. Nor is it Dad-centric. It includes leaving home and leaving the village with all its trappings, but it is more than a physical, horizontal move.

Our leaving home is *supernatural.*

It is Spirit-led.

The Spirit leads us out to the brown-pebbled banks of a swift, green river. On these banks, we meet a wide-eyed, bearded man named John. He wears camel skins pockmarked with strips of fur. And looks like he sleeps on the ground. But this John is not hiding under the water, waiting to pull us under—he's standing knee-deep in it.

John is unmoved by the crowds.

He is no "society man." He talks too loud, stands bow-legged, and stares at people. They say he eats locusts and wild honey.

Drinks water from the cactus. They say he's a prophet, but no one has seen one in generations.

Whatever he is, there is no scent of fear about him.

A few weeks earlier, a well-dressed group of professional clergy came to the River. These proud nitpickers of the Law came to henpeck, correct, and regulate. They tried dispersing the crowd—but no one paid any attention.

John spoke with fire in his words, calling them vipers and fakes and tombstones. He said their lineage was worthless, and if they didn't change, they would be chopped down with the ax. John burned and shook with such conviction that the poor men fell over backward, and scampered back to town. They haven't been to the River since.

John speaks as if possessed, his mind enraptured with something else. He talks about the same Law as the nitpickers and henpeckers do, but when John talks about it, he comes alive. Animated, as if he's holding on to a living creature.

From time to time, brave men and women approach the River.

They take John's hand and, with his help, go under. They come out of the water changed. It is some type of commitment. The crowd calls these "John's disciples." They are from all walks of life. Farmers. Fishermen. Workers. Laborers. A handful of businessmen and city leaders have even gone under the water.

On this day, another man comes to the River.

He is dressed plainly and has the well-worn look of a tradesman. He's wearing a tool belt, with loops stuffed with hammers and mallets. He's local. People recognize him by his good craftsmanship, by his work. He frames houses, works with mason and stone, makes furniture from reclaimed barn wood. There is usually a line of people waiting to have him fix things.

The man stands tall and walks straight toward John, unhurried.

For the first time, John seems nervous. He is mumbling and shaking his head in disbelief. After a brief exchange, it looks like John is refusing to take him. He says:

"I should be baptized by you! Yet you come to me?"

The carpenter says, "Yes. This is the proper time."

The man is calm. Still. He looks at John and nods.

John, who is now trembling, whispers a blessing in Hebrew. The blessing is really a cry for help. He's overwhelmed. His whole life has led to this one moment. The Passion behind his shouting, the Voice that led him to the desert, the Fire in his bones is now wrapped in flesh and skin and blood and is standing next to him in the River. His once-sure voice is shaky, as are his hands. And his eyes are rimmed with tears.

Jesus grips his biceps, as if to say, *"I'm here. You can do this."*

John nods.

With his left hand he cradles Jesus' back, and with his right, he cups his head and lowers him into the water. John lowers him into the water, lowering the One who created the waters, the earth and the stars, and then, a split second later, pulls him up again. Out of the water Jesus comes. Drenched.

He turns his palms upward, as the Spirit descends on him like a dove. He looks at John and smiles—his eyes wide and filled with fiery purpose. Suddenly, a voice from Heaven booms:

This is my son, whom I love.

This is the son of my heart.

Jesus looks once more at John, then walks out of the water, leaving his carpenter's belt and hammer lying in the sand. Then he walks east.

This is Jesus' first move on the mythic path.

His identity is shifting from the Son of Mary to the Son of the Father. Until this moment, he had been the forgotten carpenter from Nazareth, quietly pursuing his vocation, knowing his eternal destiny was approaching.

Once he goes under the water, everything changes.

He is empowered. He is identified as "Son." Then he walks into purpose.

The River is our first mythic stop.

We go to the River by leaving Mom and the village, the *vox populi*, and every expectation placed on us by others. We leave our own aspirations, dreams, and talents on the sandy shore. We are called to surrender.

The religion of the nitpickers starts with responsibility, but the vertical life of Jesus begins with *response*. We are called to the River each morning, to wait and listen patiently for the other Voice. We turn our face and palms upward; waiting for the Dove to descend, once again, on the chaos of life.

When we go under the water, this is our *threshold moment*.

When we go under the water and surrender our life, everything changes. We, like Jesus, find place with the Father.

This is the divine intention: place before purpose.

Jesus went to the River before he met the Enemy. Before his first miracle of wine at Cana. Before bringing back Lazarus from the Other Side. Before Jesus walked the lonely road to the Skull— he went under the water, and received power and affirmation of his place.

This, too, is our watery progression.

Before we are commissioned and sent. Before we heal the afflicted, feed hungry mouths, and clothe the naked. Before we father the fatherless, fight for sex-trafficked victims, confront evil and the status quo. Before we head off to work to take on the day, or love our wife or family or friends, before we create, paint, proclaim, teach, write, we—like Jesus—are called into the River.

The River is our move against the snakes, against the fury of the banshee voices. Let the winds howl and blow. Let the *vox populi* mock us and call us failures. They do not own us. They do not name us. The River is our rebellion against the *vox populi*, against the village, and against our own selfish nature.

The River is our insurrection, which according to Marquis de Lafayette, "is the most sacred of rights and the most indispensible of duties."[1]

The River brings life, freedom, and healing.

But we may identify with the crowd, standing back at a safe distance—clapping for those brave souls who wade out into the water. We make ten thousand excuses to keep from going under the River.

We need to be reminded of our true name, our name hidden with Christ in God. The Father waits for us, he waits for us to come home, to give us place. Place steadies us as we set out on the mythic path, as we cross the wind trails upon the sea. The Spirit calls us into the water—to turn and renounce our old life.

When we surrender to the Father, our old lives are buried and gone.

We are adopted as sons and daughters, into a new family, a new tribe. For those from the fatherless hut, our shame has been replaced by the dignity of divine adoption. Our internal war with the flesh, the old life is now *severed*. The impossible weight is gone, the power of death is broken, like the stone table, in two halves.

Like Jesus, we are *empowered* and *identified* at the River.

These two experiences are at the core of manhood, of who we are and who we are called to become. Above all else, we are now identified with the Father. He empowers us with his Spirit to walk the path. I get worn out along the path when I walk in my own strength and not his Spirit.

I need to hear the Father's voice.

Every day.

His words are my new vertical reality. They represent my new *place*. All of my life flows from these words, and I get off the path when I forgot who I am.

If we grew up fatherless or rejected, we have place at the River. If the world hates us, hurts and mocks us, or discriminates against us, we have place at the River. If we feel like a failure, riddled with guilt and anxiety, we have place at the River. If we are cast out by the rich cock-a-whoops or by the religious crowd, we have place at the River.

I heard these words and found place in a small chapel in Arkansas.

There were no preachers or deacons or traveling evangelists or power teams. No guilt trips or hell-raisers. No choirs or Latin poems. No one asked for my money. It was just a small gathering of college students, gathering together to sing along the shores.

For weeks, Weaver really wanted me to come with him. He lived in my dorm, two doors down. And he had this goofy, country-boy laugh. It had purity, like the laugh you had when you were young and not worried about what others think.

Weaver wasn't religious. Some college guys only wanted to talk about God and church camp. While some of them were sincere, it felt like others were reciting the Perfect Cheer. It was a weird song and dance that gave you street cred in religious circles. If Weaver knew the Cheer, he never told me or tried to make me learn it.

One time, Weaver and I were sitting in health and safety class together. The teacher was asking us morbid questions about our friends:

- How many of you have friends who would give you a finger? (Most hands went up.)
- How many have friends who would give you a kidney, if you needed it?
  (Hands went down.)
- How many of you have friends who would die for you?
  (All hands went down—I kept mine up.)

The teacher doubted. Suddenly, it felt like a setup.

"Sowers, your friend would *die* for you?" His question smacked with sarcasm.

"Yes."

"How can you be sure?" He laughed.

"Because John 15:13 says there is no greater love than he who dies for his friends. And I have a friend who loves me like that, you can ask him yourself, because he's sitting right there."

I pointed at Weaver. The teacher stared at him and frowned.

"Is this true? Would you die for Sowers?" he challenged.

Weaver's answer was barely a whisper. "Yes sir. Yes sir, I would."

The teacher wasn't smirking anymore. The class got still. There was something grave and true about his answer—there was iron in his words.

My eyes rimmed with tears. I blinked a lot, trying to keep them in.

Weaver looked at me and smiled.

A few days later, Weaver invited me to the chapel. He had been going to this singing deal and really wanted me to go. He knew I wasn't into the Perfect Cheer. But I trusted Weaver, so I told him I would go.

I arrived late, walked into the dusty chapel with two hundred other students. It smelled like old hymnals. We sat in long, dark wooden pews. Nothing fancy, no smoke machines, DJs, or lights. Everyone just sat there, quiet and calm. I hid somewhere in the back, alone. That way, if it got weird, or someone pulled out the rattlesnakes, I could bail.

A guy named Jon walked out, picked up his acoustic guitar, and started singing. I had seen Jon around; he lived next door to Weaver. He was likable. He smiled a lot, and wore calico vests over T-shirts. He bounced around on his toes when he walked. Sometimes in the hallway, he randomly hit me on the shoulder. The shoulder punch is acceptable for guys, a good substitute for hugging or other physical contact.

In the chapel, I didn't know if he was leading a concert, or if he was gonna teach me the Perfect Cheer. He didn't look grungy. But he wasn't performing or trying to impress anybody. He was a good singer, but he was kinda whisper-singing.

After a few moments watching Jon, I knew this wasn't a concert at all. It was like he didn't even notice we were there. He had his eyes closed, singing—*reaching* for something else. I looked around, suspicious. But I didn't see any weirdness.

Just normal students, wearing normal hats and carrying their normal backpacks and biology books. They were singing and reaching with Jon.

I knew these Christmas songs.

My grandmother used to take me to candlelight services on Christmas Eve. We drove to the country to a small church overlooking grass fields and oxbow lakes. We were given a white candle when we walked in the room. It was quiet and unadorned. No microphones. No marketing madness of gifts and stockings and piles of stuff. There was an eight-person choir; all were elderly. Every year, we sang the same songs and the same elderly man named Mark sang "Oh Holy Night." We listened. We sang. Just a handful of families gathered to sing and honor the dawn of redeeming grace.

At the end of the service, we lit our candles and sang "Silent Night." Standing there with my grandmother felt like we were singing on the edge of heaven, like the world was holding its breath, as we stood upon white sandy shores, and the ocean waves were lapping up to meet us. We sang and looked east and waited for the morning.

Back in the chapel, we sang with one heart.

No one cared if they were off-key. The bouncy Jon was singing with his eyes closed, singing so quietly that we could all hear ourselves sing. I think this is how it's supposed to be. When the microphones drowned out the audience, it feels more like an individual concert than collective expression.

The expression was pure. Like my grandmother's church and like Weaver's country laugh. It was not a sing-along, and it didn't feel religious. The singing had awareness and life. It had vertical direction, and was bigger than all of us. The whole room was reaching.

So I closed my eyes and joined in.

Something was happening, something I could feel. It was more than emotion, I had felt it before, but mostly walled off my heart from it. Because no one wants to be the college freshman singing guy that gets weepy. But I sang anyway. I didn't realize tears were dripping off my chin, gathering in the corner of my mouth. No one else noticed either. I didn't know why I was crying—or where the emotion was coming from. It was not something I'd felt before.

The songs had substance. They wrapped around my soul like a warm blanket, invading stone walls, like Paul and Silas's prison, breaking stone and mortar. Something broke open; something released in my soul. I had braced against it my whole life. I wasn't exactly sure at the time what was happening.

When I sang with an open heart, I was ambushed by a great affection, which was a massive surprise. As I was reaching for God, he was reaching for me. C. S. Lewis once said, "It is in the process of being worshipped that God communicates his presence to men."[2]

I'm convinced this is what happened.

My heart was coming out in streams, like a busted pipe or fire hydrant. Somehow it wasn't painful or frightening—it was all strangely comforting. I was overwhelmed by beauty and acceptance and peace.

A few minutes later, Weaver, who was sitting up front, came back to get me. He just said, "Come on." I staggered up to the front of the chapel and we prayed together. A lot of people were there praying quietly. There were no cameras; no one was pressuring me to do anything, or pushing me down, or asking me to join a church.

I don't remember what we prayed, and honestly, it didn't matter. Weaver and I were acknowledging what was happening. Jon prayed with me, too. It wasn't a religious commitment; it felt more like release.

That night in the chapel, I found acceptance. I let my guard down, began to let go of fear, of being defensive, of caring what others thought of me. As I opened my heart to God, he answered. I didn't know it then, but I was becoming a son.

I couldn't hear God speaking that night, but if I could, I think he'd have a raspy Italian accent. Like Cus D'Amato. And I think he would say:

You're my boy.

You're with me.

I need these words. Every day.

CHAPTER TEN

The Resistance

We were born to fight. To stand and stare down
Something Awful.

Something else happens at the River. Something more than acceptance and identity and place. We are clothed with power and empowered by a talisman. We are prepared and armed for our next mythic stop—for the coming fight, for our *confrontation*.

Jesus leaves the River and the Spirit leads him east, into the desert wilderness. There, he fasts for forty days, communing with the Father. He denies his flesh, relying only on the Spirit for nourishment. After he finishes fasting, the Enemy comes to tempt him, when he is famished, at his weakest.

This is Jesus' first confrontation, his first fight.

But many of us struggle with this idea of fighting.

We feel as if we have nothing to fight. Nothing to challenge our strength or wit. We live with misplaced and buried aggression. Most of my battles involve spiders, baby car seats, or getting angry at *Road Rage Guy*. Sometimes I pick a fight with automated answering machines.

This morning I killed a rogue mouse by throwing my flip-flop at it.

I suspect it's this way for a lot of us. Not only do we have nothing to fight, but we have been raised to think fighting is *bad*. Childhood fighting landed us in detention. We were warned to turn away from conflict.

Fighting lives in dark pockets, in street corners, with knife-welding muggers or rugged motorcycle thugs in seedy bars. We see the fighting spirit in athletes who dominate the gridiron on

Sundays. Or in the professionals: the warriors of the military, the twitchy boxers, and grappling MMA men who bleed for money.

Sometimes our idea is challenged.

Especially when we hear that Captain Kangaroo is actually a Marine. Or when we see the gentle pastor confronting the cussing man in Starbucks. Or when Billy Graham returns rifle fire over the heads of armed trespassers. Deep down, we know Kenny Rodgers is right: "Sometimes you have to fight when you're a man."

To be clear, I am not advocating for lunchroom bullies or online trolls who call people names, discriminate, and hate. I am not advocating for men to demean women, have short fuses, or walk around spoiling for a fight. King Solomon is right: "Better a patient man than a warrior, a man who controls his temper than one who takes a city" (Proverbs 16:32).

But we respect a man who faces his opponent without fear.

Like the young David, walking calmly onto the field to face Goliath. Like the three hundred Spartans who fought with King Leonidas in the hot gate of Thermopylae. Like those heroes who rushed the sands of Normandy, taking bullets, to save the world from a madman. These stories stir us and remind us:

Men are called to fight.

Renzo Gracie, a master black belt in Brazilian jiu jitsu, said, "Fighting is the best thing a man can have in his soul."[1]

I think Renzo is right.

Fighting is a posture of the soul. It is a learned stance. For most of us, our fighting stance is unlearned. Or it is lazy and dulled. We've been put to sleep. Chuck Palahniuk says, "We are cushioned by a make-believe, unreal world, and we have no idea what we can survive because we are never challenged or tested."

Fighting feels a long way off.

Fighting feels distant, even wrong for the meek and mild religious man. The corporate man uses all his fighter energy at work, leaving nothing for home or for himself. He comes home an empty shell, crashes down on the couch, and turns on the tube. Other men are too hurt to fight, or too burned out on life to get up off the mat. Boxing champion Jack Dempsey once said, "A champion is someone who gets up, when he can't."[2]

Fighting feels impossible for the man who lives close to Mom's pillow.

Mom argued and fought for us. And we still expect her to fight our battles, to shoulder the weight of our responsibility. This makes us passive in our relationships, at work and in life.

Fighting feels a long way off for the fatherless victim. The victim mentality says, "Life has dealt me a bad hand, a crippling blow, and there is nothing I can do about it." The victim feels he has been taken advantage of, someone has taken from him, thus he waits for another to give it back. His victim badge becomes a self-fulfilling prophecy; with no edges or boundaries, he is still victimized by others.

The wounded man is too afraid to look up. He's deathly afraid of more pain or rejection. He hates confrontation. So the bank continues to rip him off. His boss rides him. His relationship with his wife limps on. His neighbor continues to steal the morning paper. His "friends" borrow his tools and return them broken.

Passivity keeps him in check. It tells him to "stay calm, don't upset anyone." He's too afraid to build walls or say "no," as it makes others uncomfortable. He apologizes too much, and his whole life feels like one big apology.

He has no virility, no claws or teeth. No roar.

Men have forgotten how to fight.

I started taking karate when I was twelve. For years I trained and competed and worked. Later, I trained in Brazilian jiu jitsu, American boxing, and did some weapons training. At the basic level of all martial arts, instructors teach proper stance.

Japanese karate teaches to fight from the "side stance." Karate students also learn "the horse stance, the front stance, and the back stance." Later, you may learn "the cat and tiger stance." Boxers teach an open front stance, more aggressive than the side stance, but it also leaves more of your body open to be hit. The Brazilian jiu jitsu masters, Renzo, Royce, and Rickson Gracie, will tell you, "position before submission."

The legendary Bruce Lee originally studied Wing Chun Kung Fu from Ip Man. Wing Chun is about controlling the "center line." Lee fused Wing Chun with American boxing punches and footwork, training with Ali. He also mixed in some grappling and other techniques and created his own system, "Jeet Kune Do." In his book, *The Tao of Jeet Kune Do*,[3] Lee hand-draws specific fighting stances.

Stance matters.

Stance is more than a physical posture; it represents our *intention*. The victim cringes. The passive man turns away. The ashamed man looks down. But the fighter keeps his eyes wide open, and leans forward into the fight.

The fighter knows that there are times to stand and fight,

times to turn the cheek. He does both with equal ferocity. He faces every battle with courage. Some of the battles we face are:

- Emotional—Moving past our victim mentality. Working through our depression, codependency, or grief. Forgiving our father or mother.
- Relational—Fighting for our marriage. For our children. For our friends.
- Physical—Training our body. Eating the right foods. Resting.
- Spiritual—Awakening to the true, unseen battle.

The fighter is not something we can erase. It is innate; it is who we are. We can repress or deny it, or listen to the victim story. We are frustrated by conflict. But the fighter remains down below, waiting patiently for us to unlock him. While shame and passivity keep him paralyzed, love may unlock the fighter.

The first time we defend our wife, or protect our children. Or stand up to the guy who tries to rip us off. Or kick the trespassers out of our field. Or when we realize dark spiritual forces are aligned against us, to steal, kill, and destroy us.

When we realize this, something changes.

These moments change our stance.

We see in the natural. The human eye can see millions of shades of color. We trust and believe what we see. Like Elisha's servant, we despair at the coming army, at the strong force of chariots and horses riding down on top of us. But Elisha saw the invisible, and told his servant:

"Don't be afraid," the prophet answered. "Those who are with us are more than those who are with them."

And Elisha prayed, "Open his eyes, LORD, so that he may see." Then the LORD opened the servant's eyes, and he looked and saw the hills full of horses and chariots of fire all around Elisha. (2 Kings 6:16–17)

If our eyes could be opened, just for a moment, like Elisha's servant—everything would change. We would see the unseen, and no longer trust the natural. We would live in the invisible reality surrounding us. It would change our stance.

As the Enemy tempts Jesus in the wilderness, I imagine unseen legions of hags, banshees, wererats, goblins, black angels, witches, giant spiders, wraiths, beholders, mutations, and flapping bat-creatures, gathered around, following cautiously. Cackling shrill, they are giddy with evil delight. They crouch down behind the Enemy and don't dare interrupt.

The horde is in a frenzy, tripping and falling and biting each other. Stumbling along behind the Enemy, they scratch and push forward for a closer look, a closer listen. Quivering with anxious energy, they cower before the Black One. He is the Dragon and the Devourer. And he is at work now, tempting One the demons fear more than him.

The Enemy tempts Jesus in three ways:

1. He appeals to Jesus' hungry and failing flesh—*Eat!*
2. He tempts Jesus with "power"—*Bow to me, and I'll give you all this!*
3. He tells Jesus to test God—*Throw yourself down!*

Our first fight comes from within.

My human nature, the flesh, has self-destructive tendencies.

They are brought out especially when I'm hungry or lonely. Or when I am hurt or tired.

We all have earthly appetites. But when we are weak or hungry, our self-control may falter. We binge. Take a bite of the forbidden apple or swallow down gobs of Turkish delight.

Before long, self-control crumbles into nothingness and we are controlled by the urges of our flesh. The urges often go far beyond food hunger. The lusts of the flesh may be impulse purchases, sexual fantasies, social media dings, porn addiction, or escapades. We may succumb to substances, serotonin hits, alcohol, or hard drugs.

Our flesh wishes to betray us.

It is "crouching at our door, but we must master it." If we do not, little by little, it will consume us. Cracks grow into rifts, which split and fracture, until we become men with broken-down walls—slaves to our own bodies. Unless we recognize and surrender daily to the Spirit, we strive in the self-willed life, and are headed onto the lonely shores strewn with broken vessels.

This is risky conversation. On the one hand, we are eternal image bearers of God, capable of immense beauty and goodness. Because of this, we can think and speak and act as we were created.

But we are conflicted. The image of God in us has been tainted. We were not created imperfect; we were not created to die. In the tragedy of the human story, we introduced death and devastation in the Garden.

We are the fallen.

On this side of eternity, our desires are contradictions. My fleshly desires want to crop up and sneak back into the picture. I can feel this inner turmoil, this internal conflict between my old self and the new man, born of the Spirit.

Even though I am reborn, I can be a mixed bag of truths and contradictions, scars and smooth places, of shatterings and straight lines. The Apostle Paul had this same struggle. He confessed:

I am unspiritual, sold as a slave to sin. I do not understand what I do. For what I want to do I do not do, but what I hate I do. It is no longer I myself who do it, but it is sin living in me. For I have the desire to do what is good, but I cannot carry it out. For I do not do the good I want to do, but the evil I do not want to do—this I keep on doing. Now if I do what I do not want to do, it is no longer I who do it, but it is sin living in me that does it.

So I find this law at work: Although I want to do good, evil is right there with me. For in my inner being I delight in God's law; but I see another law at work in me, waging war against the law of my mind and making me a prisoner of the law of sin at work within me. What a wretched man I am! Who will rescue me from this body of death? (Romans 7:14–25)

There is an internal battle. We carry remnants from the Fall; we find evil at work in our lives. Our line between "hero" and "monster" is quite thin.

When I submit to my natural desires, the fruits of the Spirit are in absentia. They are replaced by the "weeds of the flesh," and the invisible line is crossed. There is a bitter harvest. Black weeds spring up in my heart and choke out the fruits of the Spirit. Selfishness. Discontent. Lust. Unrest. Impatience. Brutality. Pride. Tyranny. Undiscipline.

When I see these things active in my life, it makes me feel wretched. These things fall short of God's perfect design. These things grieve the Spirit, and hijack my supernatural destiny.

Our second temptation is to be *King of the Vox Populi.*

This is the popular voice, the voice of the crowd that defines truth for the masses. This voice matters more than your opinions, personal calling, or beliefs, more than your character or conviction. Walk in step with this voice—for the crowd validates your work, efforts, decisions, and your very life.

A recent poll asked youth what they want to be when they "grow up." Unlike past generations who said firemen, lawyers, doctors, and astronauts, this generation said, "Famous." They give away anything, shamelessly, for one minute of fleeting spotlight. We trade our very lives for the chance to be worshipped on the red carpet of fame.

To pursue fame is to submit to the will of the *vox populi.* Thomas Merton talks about the man who gives his life to pursue fame and world domination.

I have what you have not. I am what you are not. I have taken what you have failed to take and I have seized what you could never get. Therefore you suffer and I am happy, you are despised and I am praised, you are nothing and I am something, and I am all the more something because you are nothing. Thus, I spend my life admiring the distance between you and me.[4]

This is the proud temptation of the Pharisee to believe, "I am not like other men." This is the desire for competition and dominion. Even if the Dragon fulfills his promise and gives us the world, the cost is steep. We may lose our reputation, our mind, our health, and even our soul. We see this constantly in Hollywood starlets who flounder and flop, shedding their clothes and dignity for one chance to sit at the top of the tree.

The Enemy also tempts our trust in God. He tempts Christ to test God—by throwing himself down. "God will catch you," he says. To me, jumping off a cliff is not as powerful a temptation as eating bread. The bread feels more immediate, especially to a man who hasn't eaten in forty days.

Jesus can see the future; he knows the path he must walk. The seed of doubt has been planted, and the Enemy is hoping Jesus won't make it to the finish line.

But the core of his attack centers on River truth.

The temptation is a lot of things, but mainly, it is doubt. His assault casts doubt on our true name, our position with the Father, and our *place as sons.* Three times he asks Jesus, "If you are the Son of God, then do…" The Enemy knows if he can separate us from our true name, our identity, and our place, we will derail. Oftentimes, his work is finished after that—we simply destroy ourselves.

We live in a real supernatural battle. Sometimes we believe the battle is in the here and now, like Peter, we chop an ear off the guard. But we miss it. Jesus later said to Pilate, "My kingdom is not of this world, if it were, my servants would fight to prevent my arrest" (John 18:36). Peter was wrong. The Crusades were wrong. As is every other wing nut who uses religion as an excuse for physical violence.

The true war is not against other men or terrorism or drugs or corporate greed. Our fight is the unseen, hidden battle. Ephesians 6:12 says: "Our battle is not against flesh and blood, but against the rulers, against the authorities, against the powers of this dark world and against the spiritual forces of evil in the heavenly realms."

One: We are in a battle.

Two: The battle is invisible and spiritual, with dark forces of evil.

I think if we could see the invisible, only for a moment, we would wake up. Our great danger is to "have sight but no vision," and live only in the natural. Sure, the devil may exist, but he doesn't hang out in my suburb. He wears red stretchy pants and only comes out during Mardi Gras.

Make no mistake: The Dragon is as real as the chair you sit on, as the book you read, as the oxygen you breathe. Until we live in this reality, our posture will be off. We live ignorant of the truth, and remain exposed and vulnerable. Reformer Martin Luther said, "I was born to fight devils and factions. It is my business to remove obstructions, to cut down thorns, to fill up quagmires, and to open and make straight paths."[5]

We, like Martin Luther, were born to fight.

We start by seeing we are in a battle. We start by being *watchful.*

This is Jesus at Gethsemane.

Golgotha was looming large in his mind. A bloody death at the Skull was his destiny. Jesus knew the future, every detail of what was to come, and was overwhelmed. He was sorrowful to the point of death. These were his last "free" moments. Soon the traitor and the mob would come. In his last free moments, he asked his friends to watch and pray with him in the garden. He prayed and stressed and sweated blood. The first task of the spirit warrior is to watch and pray. Thomas Jefferson once said:

"The price of freedom is eternal vigilance."[6]

We have two choices: To sleep like the disciples in the garden, or to watch and pray. Whatever the day has in store for us, be it storms or battles or victories or celebrations, we must be intently watchful, we must stop and pray, as Jesus did in the garden. Matthew picks up on this: "Watch and pray so that you will not fall into temptation. For the spirit is willing but the flesh is weak" (26:41).

We are to watch. To be vigilant.

The battle is at our doorstep.

But we are not defenseless.

Ephesians 6:11 describes our armor and proper fighting stance. It says, "Put on the full armor of God, so when the day of evil comes, you may be able to stand your ground." It shows us how to stand in the face of an onslaught. It describes our battle armor, the things we put on in preparation for the battle. Belt of truth. Breastplate of righteousness. Feet in the gospel of peace. Shield of faith. Helmet of salvation. Romans 13:12 says, "The night is nearly over, the day is almost here. So let us put aside the deeds of darkness and put on the armor of light."

We are clothed with power, encased with supernatural armor of light. We are called to stand. We do this by watching and praying. Our stance changes from apathy to awareness. We are now awake and prepared for the fight, long before the battle engulfs us. And we are not unarmed.

The talisman we receive comes in the form of a dove.

CHAPTER ELEVEN

A Living Flame

The Spirit changes us into fire. This is our transformation.

The mythic talisman comes in many forms. Aegis, the shield. Mjölnir, the hammer. Or Narya, the fiery ring. Our talisman is a razor-sharp, double-edged sword. It is otherworldly. It has divine power to pierce through the natural and affect the supernatural, demolishing strongholds and severing darkness.

We are called to take up the "sword of the Spirit," which is the word of God. It is a finely honed blade, able to pierce through soul and spirit. And it is forged by the breath of God (see Hebrews 4.12, 2 Timothy 3.16). But sometimes it's hard to know how to wield this talisman. This is where a mentor or mythic elder often steps in.

We long to sit in the Circle of Elders.

Sometimes there are none. There are no bearded elders inviting us to take a seat on the ground and drink the ancient draughts. But there is another tribe, another mythic group waiting for us. As Martin Shaw suggests, "a third of community could live entirely in our imagination."[1]

This could be the rhythmic jazz-poems of Langston Hughes. The sober notes of a Highland bagpipe echoing across green hills. A country singer from Arkansas telling his story in *The Man Comes Around*. A fiery prophet standing up to King Ahab. A group of writers sitting in an Oxford pub named The Eagle and The Child.

My mentor was a silver-haired, hawk-eyed man named Bill Smith.

Bill Smith showed up at the door of my mom's house with two other men named Bill. Bill Sr. is a pastor, and Bill Jr. was one of my high school buds, and is now a pastor. I was home on Christmas break, and had just finished my first semester of college.

Providence, it seems, aligned our meeting.

Days before I met Bill, I was singing Christmas carols with Weaver and Jon. I had just experienced God in the Chapel. I was being stirred, and called into the world of men, out of the village and into the swamps. I was called by both Spirit and Elder.

After pleasantries with Mom, we loaded up the car with shotguns, waders, camo, duck calls, and drove to Stuttgart. Stuttgart is the home of "Riceland," which means it's chock-full of rice fields. Every winter, hundreds of thousands of ducks migrate down the Mississippi flyway. Tons of them stop off in Stuttgart to fatten up on rice. And the hunters are waiting.

Bill owned a cabin outside Stuttgart, in the heart of the Mississippi River Delta. It was a rustic, bare-boned thing. It sat on a ridge overlooking flooded timber and fields. The inside had antlers and skulls and mounted wood ducks.

That night, we ate venison stew and crunchy, misshapen biscuits. Drank tea out of mason jars. After dinner, we sat around blowing duck calls. I used a double-reed call, a Duck Commander. As I was doing my best duck impersonation, Bill was doing a good job watching and cheering. We all took turns, and Bill was solid on his call.

Then Bill shared his story.

He managed money for some high-flying clients. He was rich, but unhappy. He owned everything and nothing. Something was missing, so he looked for relief in substances. But neither money nor drink satisfied him. His life crumbled. Bill raised the white flag. In desperation, he prayed and asked God for help.

God listened.

Bill died to his old self. Died to everything that was killing him. Everything he owned was owning him. Bill realized life was more than a job or the contents of his wallet. His eyes were opened and he embraced a new, vertical reality. Bill stopped living for himself and stuff; instead he became radically generous.

When Bill shared his story, he came alive. His eyes had stars shining in them. As I listened to him share, I was impressed that a man of his stature and business acumen could be so devoted to spiritual things. Bill was a man of intense conviction. Then, out of nowhere, Bill stared at me with those brown hawk-eyes and asked:

"John, what kind of man do you want to be?"

I had no idea. None.

I stammered around, making indecipherable grunting noises. I wanted to give Bill the right answer. To be honest, I hadn't even thought about it. The question made me feel like a failure, because I didn't have an answer. So I looked down at my feet and mumbled through something about being a good man, a husband, and a dad.

Bill's answer surprised me:

"Well, that's a good start. I'd love to help you with that."

For the next ten years, he did.

That weekend in Stuttgart, we talked about success, how God's idea for it is different than ours. This was a far cry from my life vision. I secretly wanted to play for the Boston Red Sox. But I was already seeing the improbability in this. I was good in high school, All-State and all that, but in college, everyone was All-State. I was decent in college, but Dustin Pedroia I was not.

Until that point, no man had sat down with me and talked about the future. I had wild ideas. If baseball didn't work out, I would be a professional hunter. Or a personal trainer or body-guard. Who knows?

Bill told me that success was not playing professional sports, or making a million dollars. Not about being a rock star or own-ing a bunch of stuff. Our eternal destiny was found with God. This new idea sounded good, but I had zero idea how to do it.

We started memorizing verses together, Joshua 1:8 and Psalm 1. He was teaching me how to use the Sword of the Spirit. Teach-ing me to hold everything in my life up to the Bible. Whatever areas are off or mismatched, those places need our attention, our prayers, and the grace of God.

Bill told me that success was loving God.

He said if I surrendered and set my heart on God, he would lead me. My life would be like a fruitful tree, planted by the River, a tree that does not see decay. This shaped my definition and vision of manhood.

Bill gave me direction, saying my life would prosper if I held it up to the word of God. Until then, I had no idea what manhood was or how to get there. He laid out a blueprint for me. Told me if I followed and obeyed God, my life would prosper. I would avoid all sorts of traps and pitfalls, and would be free from the pres-sures of the world.

For the first time, I didn't feel lost.

Bill helped me take my first steps. We memorized the Scrip-tures together. We read the Proverbs and talked about wisdom. That next semester, Bill invited me to his house to read a book he wrote called *A Man and His Word*. Every week, I drove the two-hour round-trip to attend. The men in the group were thirty to forty years older than me, and they had been in the Elder Circle for a long time.

But they were pretty normal. They drove normal cars. Wore normal clothes. Khaki pants. Polo shirts. None of them had beards, piercings, or ink. Someone told his story. The men opened up about their families and their struggles at work or home. Even though I was a greenhorn, they welcomed me into their Circle.

It was the first time I felt accepted by the Circle of Elders. Before, acceptance from men was conditional; it was from boss-dads and baseball coaches.

Every week, I watched as Bill led those men around the coffee table. Sometimes we got down on our knees to ask God for help. I had never prayed on my knees before. We wouldn't always just "blurt out" prayers; sometimes we would listen and wait and be patient and still. We shared honestly and openly. I heard these elders call out to God with loud and sincere voices. Sometimes with broken voices.

Several years later, when Bill found out I was attending Trinity in Chicago, he wanted to pay for it. He paid for my graduate school and wrote me letters while I was there. One letter said, *"You are a man. And I'm proud of you."*

It was the first time a man told me that.

I still have that letter.

Bill stayed in touch throughout college—writing lettings, and taking me hunting or fishing when I was in Little Rock. He asked solid questions and then spent hours listening to me. We talked about "romance and finance." He didn't overwhelm me with correction, advice, or religious responses; he let me come to my own conclusions.

Over the next few months, my friends and teammates noticed the difference.

My life was changing as I encountered the Spirit. Bill talked about staying connected to God, as he is the Vine and we are the branches (see John 15:1–5). When we are connected to the Vine, we see fruit. The things of the Spirit were activated: Love. Joy. Peace. Patience. Gentleness. Kindness. Goodness. Self-Control. (See Galatians 5:22.)

As I surrendered my life to the Spirit of God, I was being transformed.

This was more than religion or going to church or do-good moralism. Our spiritual lives may go this route, but it is small. It is a cheap imitation, a bumper-sticker reductionism of what is truly possible.

Our vertical life can be a little rule and a little prayer. This is neat and tidy. Controllable. This life reduces spirituality to an hour and a half on Sunday morning. To giving 10 percent to the church. Being a goodly man.

Or we may choose the more dangerous route, fully yielding ourselves to the talisman, the word of God which is a "consuming fire" (Deuteronomy 4:24, Hebrews 12:29). As we yield our lives to this reality, we are *transformed*.

Richard Foster tells this story:

A young Abbot once came to an Elder and asked, "Father, according as I am able, I keep my little rule, my little fast, my prayer and my meditation. And according as I am able, I strive to keep my heart clean, now what more should I do?"

The Elder rose up in reply and stretched out his hands to heaven, and his fingers became like ten lamps of fire. He said, "Why not be totally changed into fire?"[2]

As we wield the sword, the sword begins to wield us.

Our life begins to match its rhythm. Our life is blended with the fire of the Spirit. For he is a fire, and his word is also like fire, a hammer that breaks the rock into pieces. (See Jeremiah 23:29.) This holy fire purifies us and refines us into his image.

This is our transformation.

The first thing I feel when I get close to a forge is intense heat. The forge is basically an oven to heat a steel billet past 1,500 degrees so it can be shaped into a knife or a sword. When a billet is heated past this critical temperature, it can then be molded, hammered on the anvil, and shaped into a blade. Not only does the outer shape change, but so do the fiber and the grain of the steel.

You take the billet out of the forge and it is glowing hot, red or white. Then it can be placed on the anvil to reshape. Using hammer and muscle, the steel is now pliable; it may be flattened, compressed, and bent to the knife maker's will. Once the piece has been shaped, it is quenched in water or oil to harden the edge and then heat-tempered to make sure it is not brittle.

In Japanese sword making, the best samurai swords are folded nearly twenty times, reforged, and hammered. The edge is differentially quenched with clay, and it is razor-sharp, while the back of the sword is extremely pliable. If the entire sword was as hard as the edge, it would break quickly. But if the edge was as soft as the spine, it would not hold. Modern engineers praise Japanese swords as the ultimate achievement, as they bring out the characteristics of the metal so it can perform in the highest possible way.

Our lives are this way.

Peter talks about the "refiner's fire," but until I started working with steel, I had no context for what he meant. I had no idea how hot the forge is and how much a piece of steel changes in the process. It takes careful thought, time, and work.

Most of us want to steer clear of the fires of the forge. We want to avoid the hammer and anvil. But it is in these very places where we are purified and shaped into our eternal destiny.

The Bible talks about the word of God as a divine weapon, a weapon not like the weapons of the world. It has "divine power to demolish strongholds" (2 Corinthians 10:4). Meditating, forging our lives on the anvil of the word of God, gives the Holy Spirit a vocabulary to work in us internally, as well as to speak into the lives of others.

Also, we see David describe the praise of God as a "double-edged sword in their hands" (Psalm 149:6). We know singing to God is somehow connected to being filled with the Spirit (see Ephesians 5:18–19), and it was victorious and faithful singing that brought down the walls of Jericho.

We need these weapons.

More than carrying weapons, our life must become one.

For the man who goes into the forge and onto the anvil, his life is changed. The man who surrenders to the Consuming Fire welcomes the sweat and strain, as he is being re-formed into something sharp and powerful and deadly. His very life is put into the forge—fire pressed and cold hammered into something else entirely.

This is our *transformation*.

As we step into the Consuming Fire, we become, in the words of Robert Murray M'Cheyne: "awful weapons."[3] We become living flames and servants of the true Fire that burned before the creation of the world. We are in the process of becoming either "immortal horrors or everlasting splendors." Our lives are transformed into the image of Christ as we set our hearts and affections on him. We burn white-hot and become more like him as we set our hearts and affections upon him.

There are days when I avoid the fire. Days when my edge is blunted. Days when I feel more of an "ignoble vessel" than a noble one. There are days when my life looks more like a blocky steel billet than an awful weapon, forged by the Master.

Too often, I fail to hear his voice over the deafening noise of my life. I habitually step into a frenetic, adrenaline pace, filling my life with noise, hurry, and crowds. And then I feel victimized by the rush. "*I just don't have time.*"

I turn a deaf ear to his voice when I bury myself under layers of blogs, texts, posts, tweets, and e-mails. Noise. Over time, my life begins to align with the shallow buzz of adrenaline, social media, and coffee. I slip into this rhythm for weeks, weeks which become months, which become years.

I don't notice the difference, at least for a while.

But slowly and steadily, my soul conforms to a panicked-induced pace, and I move further and further from the core. My life becomes less about living and more about reacting, an ADD reaction to the swarming, digital madness.

Frantic banshee voices scream at me:

Be this! Think that! Consume more!

Consume this image, become this image. Buy this shoe, become this athlete. Buy this truck, become a truck man. Buy this purse, become a shining actress.

This is the empty language of idol worship.

Empty your bank accounts. Buy more stuff. Hoard.

And when everything to spend has been spent, keep spending into debt. You are what you own and you can never own enough. Worship the worthless idol, until you yourself become worthless. Black Elk whispers to us: "Any man attached to things of this world lives in ignorance and is being consumed by the snakes of his own passions."[4]

When I live for idols, my perspective changes, my vision shrinks, and my passion dies.

I am prone to wander and to worry. Prone to have guilt over yesterday or anxiety over tomorrow. Like Narcissus, I fall in love with my own reflection, and stop living for others. People are dehumanized and become objects of my desire, or "contacts" used to advance my agenda.

When I stray far from the Fire, my perspective changes, and so does my character. The weeds of the flesh begin to bloom. And there is a growing distance between who I am and who I am called to be. C. S. Lewis says this dilemma is normal. He says other voices are rushing at me like a screaming hobgoblin:

It comes the very moment you wake up each morning. All your wishes and hopes for the day rush at you like wild animals. And the first job each morning consists simply in shoving them all back; in listening to that other Voice, taking that other point of view, letting that other larger, stronger, quieter life come flowing in. And so on, all day.

Standing back from all your natural fussings and frettings; coming in out of the wind.[5]

The wild animals must be pushed aside.

Our natural fussings and frettings must be put to death. Paul says this in Colossians 3:5: "Put to death therefore, whatever belongs to your earthly nature." And in Romans 8:13: "If you live according to the flesh, you will die. But if, by the Spirit, you put to death the misdeeds of the body, you will live."

This is the **Death-Life**.

It's one thing to sing and pray and have the best intentions. It is quite another thing to stop and surrender, to raise the white flag daily, and to be a servant of the Secret Fire. This is the daily rhythm of the Death-Life. This is Jesus' call in Luke 9:23 when he says, "If any man wishes to come after me, let him deny himself, take up his cross daily and follow me."

We naturally resist surrender, opting for the illusion of control, wishing to be competent and self-sufficient. But the Cross requires us to admit our need, to turn a deaf ear to these voices, and shove them all back. When we walk the Death-Life, we are transformed into fire, and join the ranks of *Bearded Men* who have gone before us. We walk the hallowed halls, alongside men who:

Through faith, conquered kingdoms, fought for justice, shut the mouths of lions, quenched the fury of the flames, escaped the edge of the sword, whose weakness was turned to strength; and who became powerful in battle and routed foreign armies. Others who were tortured, refusing to be released so that they might gain an even better resurrection.

Some faced jeers and flogging, and even chains and imprisonment. They were put to death by stoning; they were sawed in two; they were killed by the sword. They went about in sheepskins and goatskins, destitute, persecuted and mistreated—*and the world was not worthy of them.* (Hebrews 11:33–38)

We see this shift happen in Jesus, from Gethsemane to Golgotha. In the garden, he was overwhelmed to the point of death. But he went to the cross "for the joy set before him" (Hebrews 12:2). Jesus endured the crushing pain, the nails, the thorny crown, the scorn and shame, seeing the risen life beyond.

Jesus entered the Battle at Golgotha with joy.

He died. Then rose in glory.

He was crushed. Pierced. Bloodied. As he walked, he carried the shame of the world upon his shoulders but his heart was *singing.*

This is the heroic path of Jesus, the joyous walk from village to the Skull.

There and back again. Christ faced the Dragon in the desert and then faced him again, himself and the world, at Golgotha. He prepared for this fight by spending the night in watchful and bloody prayer.

In the garden of Gethsemane, Christ set his eyes on the final conflict—the cross. He was battle ready. Ready to carry the wounds which would bring many to glory. To offer his life for ours, even if it meant being pierced and crushed. The force of this single act tore the curtain of time.

But he didn't stop at Golgotha.

Buried and left and hidden behind the guarded stone, he

waited for three days. But his love is unstoppable, burning eternal. Many waters cannot quench it; it is undeterred by death or hell. Stronger than graves, his love does not decay. Love's roar echoes down the halls of time.

Unrestrained by the bonds of death, Jesus rose from the grave. The resurrection is the penultimate act of history.

This is Tolkien's *Eucatastrophe*[6]—the swift and sudden turning, from darkness and death into light and life. It is when the moment of utter darkness becomes the failing of the Enemy. It is when all hope is lost, when we are surrounded by the horde army, and suddenly a rising tide comes and sweeps them all away. We see the Eucatastrophe in Peter's disbelief at the Tomb, when the angel tells Peter:

"He is not here, he is risen."

When Christ rose from the dead, I believe the morning stars sang once again, as they did in Creation. The angels stomped and danced, shouted wildly and cheered for joy. The noise was brilliant, racing swiftly over the earth as pounding waves crashed onto the morning shores, as tangles of wildflowers opened over the spring fields, as skies were colored and streaked by a thousand rising suns.

Skulls and Songs
by John Sowers

Aghast! Along the gaping wound,
Blood flows and becomes a mighty swoon
dripping, flowing, while terror ignorant, is gloating.
Bitter fumes choke the land, weaving malice unabated,
against one life lost, underrated.

Corpses buckle, claw and struggle, climb into living,
wretched and rotting flesh sees new beginnings.
Drunk with madness all flee the woe,
the final end to life's gnashing misery—behold!

Ere this end is mere beginning,
of things foretold by those who longed to see
the winning, unfold, the Grand Songs

Forever singing, to the Firstborn and Last,
who conquered death by drinking,
the cup of grief that we, too,
may hear the Song of Life and sing.

Jesus conquered death.

His Death-Life is now our joyous opportunity. "And if the Spirit of him who raised Jesus from the dead is living in you, he who raised Christ from the dead will also give life to your mortal bodies because of his Spirit who lives in you" (Romans 8:11).

Jesus invites us to lose our lives, take up the cross daily and follow him. As we do, we find his risen life and our eternal destiny.

This is our glorious standard.

It reminds me of the Battle of Pelennor Fields, where the Rohirrim are grossly outnumbered. They cannot win. But they ride down on the dark host anyway. They charge into certain death, giving their lives with joy, with chanting and singing.

> For morning came, morning and a wind from the sea; and the darkness was removed, and the hosts of Mordor wailed, and terror took them, and they fled and died, and the hoofs of wrath rode over them. And then all the hosts of Rohan burst into song, and they sang as they slew, for the joy of battle was upon them, and the sound of their singing that was fair and terrible came even to the City.[7]

If we put our ear to the ground and listen closely, we may still hear their hoofbeats, battle horns, and their chanting:

> *Arise, arise, Riders of Théoden!*
> *Fell deeds awake: fire and slaughter!*
> *spear shall be shaken, shield be splintered,*
> *a sword-day, a red day, ere the sun rises!*
> *Ride now, ride now! Ride to Gondor![8]*

CHAPTER TWELVE

There and Back Again

The men who change history are those
who love well.

Whealen you ride home from the wild, everything has changed. The Secret Fire lights your eyes and simmers in your bones. You are coiled steel, burning with quiet intensity. Your life has a tempered, clay-hardened edge. You have been put into the fire and onto the anvil, and your old life has died.

When a man embraces the Death-Life, he no longer cares for the *vox populi*. He cares not for its ridicule or scorn or mockery, for its praise or flattery. He doesn't care if his business is featured in the local paper, if he is despised by peers or honored by strangers. He steps out of the social media race, not worrying if his blog trends or if his Facebook page has enough "Likes." He is unmoved.

When he opens his mouth, people listen. There is iron in his words. Like John, he makes people nervous; they cannot deny his edge or his truth. The crowd has no edge, as they wait for the popular voice to define the ever-changing truth.

The doubters scoff and question: "Isn't this just the boy from nowhere?"

But this fiery man answers to no one.

The village feels threatened by us. We don't know it, but we now have the intense look of a *Bearded Man*. We are fearless and dangerously alive. Our senses are heightened. We are aware now, of the chanting crows, warning us of ill omens. Of the widow struggling to sell her wares so her children may have bread. Of the wind chimes signaling the coming thunderstorm. Of the wolf-dog sleeping in the market, wanting to jump the hedge and join his pack. We understand his desperation.

Our return home rarely feels like a welcome one.

In earlier days or in other cultures, the village recognized us for what we are. Maasai warrior. Windwalker. Orc hunter. Spartan. Comanche. The historical village was conditioned to recognize and celebrate the boy's transitional passage into manhood. They understood the significance and necessity of the boy's initiation, and how it edifies the greater community.

Traditionally, the Circle of Elders heralded our return. They welcomed us, gave us responsibility and room to lead, and sometimes, bowed to us. But instead of a Circle, we find a village who shuns and mocks us, save a curious few. This makes our *return* to the village one of the hardest parts on the mythic path.

Today's return to the village often involves more conflict.

Our village, like Iron John's, is hostile to the *Hairy Man*. Some are hostile to the idea of manhood altogether. Recently, a customer in an American restaurant politely asked to go to the men's room. A seemingly normal question. But the waiter responded in anger, "We don't recognize male or female here; choose your own way."

Not only do we face conflict in the woods but also from the *vox populi*. They are hostile to our very existence. To them, we should shave. And keep our voice down. The extremists bully us with the stones of ridicule or "outrage." They threaten us to be quiet. In extreme cases, they call for us to be locked in an iron cage.

The village is terrified of the Secret Fire.

Many men live for the unfulfilled fantasy of village approval.

We are afraid to roar, afraid if we do, the village will ridicule us. Most likely, they will.

But our final act, our mission from the Gray King, is to walk into the center of town, climb the watchtower, and *ring the bell*. We are to awaken the sons of long-dead knights, rousing sleep-walking men, men who are tiptoeing safely down to the grave.

We ring the bell by living what we learned in the woods. We ring the bell by claiming our mythic ground. When a man claims his mythic ground, he reroutes history. Sir Thomas Carlyle wrote, "The history of the world is but the biography of great men."[1]

One of these men was buried on June 2, 1996.

Christian de Chergé was buried with six of his friends. Their simple caskets were borne by armed soldiers. Ten thousand people gathered to bear witness to their legacy, honoring their memory at the Trocadero in France, just across from the Eiffel Tower.

The seven men were monks serving the Algerian people.

They gardened. Tended bees and sick villagers.

Even though the monks were different from their Islamic neighbors, their friendship grew. The country had welcomed the monks for over fifty years. And the monks, for their part, acted as quiet servants, healers, friends. The monks and their neighbors were like a married couple, which, despite their differences, had grown together with time, seeing the richness in the differences.

Following the assassination of the Algerian president, groups of radical Muslim terrorists filled the leadership void. Soon, they threatened to kill all foreigners if they did not leave Algeria.

The monks were forced to make a decision:

Flee the country and live, or stay and face certain death.

To leave meant to abandon their neighbors, friends, and the place they'd long called home. To leave meant abandoning a country that forbade speaking the gospel, but long embraced the small group of men who humbly lived it. Their Algerian neighbors were afraid, but also needed the monks now more than ever. One woman added, "If you go away, you will rob us of your hope and we will lose ours."

To a man, the monks resolved to stay.

Personally, I've never lived under the threat of death. But one time, I was convinced someone was in the house. We heard noises upstairs and found the back door open. I grabbed a hatchet and called the police. They searched every room. Even though they didn't find anyone, I was charged with adrenaline and uncertainty.

I think the monks probably felt this way constantly. They couldn't sleep well. Every nightly noise could be an armed intruder. Every conversation at the local market or medical clinic could be with a terrorist. Even if they tried to remain calm, their nerves had to be frayed to shreds.

Soon the violence hit close to their home.

Just two miles from the monastery, a group of Croatian workers were ambushed and found with their throats slit. They were working for the state, building a water reservoir—not tourists or reporters or people that usually drew hostility. They were contracted by Algeria to help Algerians. And they were still killed.

The message of the dead Croatians was clear: No one was safe.

Government officials begged the monks to leave or accept protection. They thought to stay meant collective suicide.

But the monks refused to leave.

And they could not accept protection, as no weapons could be allowed in the monastery, nor did they want to align themselves with any side in the conflict.

Weeks later, armed terrorists stormed the monastery dressed as police officers, asking for the "pope" of the house. As Brother Christian walked out to meet his death, he was not afraid. Rather, he was outraged. Terrorists had brought weapons into the monastery. So he rebuked them:

No one has ever come in with a weapon into this house of peace. Both your religion and mine forbid weapons in a place of worship. If you want to talk here, you must leave your weapon outside the building. Otherwise, we must go outside.[2]

The group walked outside to the courtyard, where the statue of Mary stood with open arms, an unconditional gesture of welcome. Christian spoke with Sayah Attia, the executioner of the Croatians and the terrorist leader of the region.

Sayah had three demands:

1. He wanted medical care for his men.
2. He wanted to take medicine and money.
3. He wanted to take a monk to doctor his men in the field.

Christian denied his requests. But he did offer to help if the men went to the monks' medical clinic and received treatment like everyone else.

Surprisingly, Sayah accepted.

The monks let out a collective exhale.

And as Christian took Sayah out of the monastery, he added, "You know, this is Christmas Eve. This is when we celebrate the birth of Jesus, the Son of Mary, whom we call the Prince of Peace."

"Excuse me, I didn't know," Sayah replied, shocked at the reproach.

Then the two men shook hands.

But with the New Year came a new dawn of violence.

Hundreds of people were being killed every week. Religious leaders—both Christian and Muslim—were being targeted for the first time. The monks prayed again about leaving, as they didn't want to be committing suicide by staying. They knew death was near. They came out of the prayer time with new resolve.

One monk added, "If I leave here, I leave myself."

Weeks later, seven of the brothers were kidnapped, killed, and beheaded.

The next day, forty thousand churches throughout Europe rang their bells.

The funeral was attended by scores of high-ranking government officials, spiritual leaders, and hundreds of ordinary Algerians. At the funeral, Father Olivera said:

There are times to speak and times to be quiet. After fifty years of silence, our seven brothers have become spokesmen for the stifled voices and anonymous individuals who have given their lives for a more humane world. They showed we must enter the world of others, be that other a Christian or a Muslim. For if "the other" does not exist, there can be no love of the other. These men were manifestations of the

Gospel—a life freely given in the spirit of love is never a life lost, but one found again in Him who is Life.[3]

Following the service, the crowd slowly filed past the coffins. Muslims and Christians alike mourned. Some gently held the monks' pictures, while others whispered tender good-byes.

Later, they found a letter written by Brother Christian. He wrote it in anticipation of his death. In the letter, Christian *forgives* his soon-to-be murderer. He writes:

If it should happen one day that I become a victim of terrorism, I want my community, my church, and my family to remember, my life was given to God and Algeria. I ask them to accept the One Master of all life, who was not a stranger to this brutal departure. I would ask them to pray for me, for how could I be worthy of such an offering?

And to you, my Last-Minute Friend, who will have known not what you are doing, I want this thank you and goodbye to be, a God-bless for you also. Because in God's face I see yours. May we meet again as happy thieves in Paradise, if it pleases God, the Father of us both.

Sacrificial love is the heart of manhood.

It is our offering and legacy. It is the thread connecting the worlds of fairy and myth, history and legend. These perilous lands are filled with ordinary men who were thrust into the arresting extraordinary. These men, like Brother Christian, made the choice to give their lives for the greater good. And they became heroes.

The men who change history are those who love well.

Rather than choosing the path of least resistance, they chose the other, often at great cost to themselves. They forsook the paths of selfishness, of fear and cowardice.

And they became heroes. You see these men every day: Faithful dads. Husbands. Soldiers. Workers. Mentors. Servants. Friends.

Love spirals through them onto us. And we are changed. There are generations of everyday heroes who have gone before us: parents, relatives, friends, and others—who gave away their lives in the name of love. These are the quiet heroes—changing history without pomp, and without fanfare. Without paparazzi.

These men are the protagonists of history. They are the centerpieces of the great stories, stories that focus on one who gives his life away. This is the enduring testimony of the Cross of Jesus. Nothing stirs us and moves history more than sacrificial love. Nothing. There is no greater love.

Love is not a fleeting emotion that evaporates at dawn. This is our current definition of love, as portrayed by Hollywood. Love is something you can "fall in or out of," like a hidden pit. We are passive recipients of love. And if we "fall out of it," it excuses all kinds of monstrosities. Love, according to C. S. Lewis, "is something more stern and more splendid than kindness."

Love is seen in the undying testimony of Brother Christian, whose life echoes the words of the Apostle Paul: "For to me, to live is Christ and to die is gain" (Philippians 1:21). Christian's life was given to God long before he died in the monastery. He walked the Death-Life and gave himself to the One "who was not a stranger to this brutal departure." He felt unworthy to die in the name of Love. Rather, he called himself a happy thief in Paradise.

Our temptation is to read a story about Christian and treat it like fiction. Or like a feature film. In our minds, we stand outside the story, as interested observers. But we don't see ourselves as active participants in the story, or as main characters. We cannot fathom being in the lead role. "Amazing story," we think, "but I would *never* do that. If terrorists threatened me, I would be long gone."

But love is stronger than death.

The love of Christ compels us (see 2 Corinthians 5:14).

His love activates us into movement. It stiffens our backbone, triumphs over terror, hardens our resolve, and leads us through Korengal—the valley of death. His love guides us through the dark night. Gives us the fortitude to stand unflinchingly before the clawed hand of the Enemy. Our motivation to be great dads and great men is not religious guilt, or spiritual debt, or even something better, such as gratitude to God. Our highest motivation is the overwhelming love of Christ.

Love never fails.

Love is not quenched by oceans, or extinguished by fear. Love compelled Salvatore to run into a wall of gunfire. Love held Christian to the country and people he loved. Love drove my fear of being a dad right out of the hospital.

That first night my girls were born, I didn't know the next step. I stayed awake most of the night. Full of adrenaline, I watched Rosie and Little Bird like a hawk. I felt afraid and exposed. I could hear Something Awful bumping about in the next room. He convinced me the stork delivered the babies to the wrong man. With no clue how to be a dad, I was an accident waiting to happen.

So I opened my heart and wrote down my fears.

I never set out to write a book about bears or bearded men or elves. I hadn't discovered how myth could guide me into the harbor of manhood. It started as a journal entry, written while sitting on a hospital bed, the night my girls were born. Kari was rightly exhausted and fast asleep. I didn't share it with anyone for months. When I finally did, it connected. Men laughed and were nodding right along with me. They *knew*. They knew what it felt like to be lost. They knew what it felt like to be Murdock.

This encouraged me to keep writing. I wrote what I felt, even though I had not yet been to the haunted woods. I had never seen a Kodiak. I didn't know the mythic steps. Nor did I have a conclusion. My goal was honesty.

The first months of fatherhood, I was in survival mode. Trying not to put diapers on backward. Learning how to swaddle and shampoo a baby's head. Trying to be the best husband and dad I could be, although I didn't have a measuring stick or a map.

I didn't write from a position of strength, or from the popular *Bravado Man* idea. I wasn't a Navy SEAL or a UFC champion. I don't own a Harley and I never won a Heisman. I think most man-books are written by guys who are barrel chested and have deeper voices than me. My writing was less flexing, and more confessing.

I listened and scribbled. The words came slowly, but freely. They were tinged with fear, but also determination. Like the rising tide, they came farther and farther upon the shore, then back out to the sea. I connected to the words of C. S. Lewis when he said, "*I never exactly made a book. It's rather like taking dictation.*"[4]

As I started unpacking ideas such as sacrifice, place, wildness, and being married to Mom, I was writing my own experience.

It felt like I was also confessing for a generation of men without place, a generation of men who, like me, feel inadequate and confused.

God met me in my inadequacy.

My confidence began to grow as a man, as a husband and dad. While on Kodiak Island, God opened my eyes to the mythic steps. Through my conversation with Lewis and Tolkien, I saw mythic heroes following the same path—severance, confrontation, transformation, return.

These myths informed and shaped cultures, written and told by tribes with initiation passages for manhood. But the more I read, the more I realized that our Western world has no initiation rites for young men. We have no vision or *language* for it. The mythic rhythms steered me, as Tolkien said, to the True Harbor. The Christ story is our one true Myth—"where history and legend have met and fused."

The Christ story informs our journey, our own initiation passage.

As I began to unpack this idea, I found confidence and direction. No longer did I need to meander; I found the path. I considered rewriting the first chapter, as I was ashamed at its inadequate voice. But it was my honest voice.

As I explored the true Myth, I began to see the clear path, both for myself and for the reader. I began walking, and I started to change. My writing voice changed. I woke up to the coho stirring, and with each step, I felt more alive. Like the song "Radioactive," by Imagine Dragons,[5] I felt it "in my bones, enough to make my system run."

I was empowered to venture out from the village. I knew it was a man's destiny to leave home and get into real trouble. To step out of comfort and into the haunted woods, and face Something Awful. Once I faced my fears, by the grace of God, I walked away transformed. I returned ready to give away my passion and my life. Now I feel the strength and confidence to fully offer myself to others.

This momentum translated into doing something about my physical health. It was a confrontation I had avoided. I had tried before but the New Year's resolutions had failed. I knew something deeper had to happen. Something more than getting the right plan, trying the Paleo diet, joining a gym and doing a ton of push-ups, sit-ups, and planks.

I needed something deeper. I needed to make a clean break, an inner severance from the routine and the despair. It was about taking back control. Instead of being passive, I started leaning into life.

I started by eliminating wheat. Wheat is in a surprising amount of food. I learned the bleached, enriched variety is especially bad. After cutting out wheat for a few weeks, the fog in my mind started to clear. I had more energy. My stomach shrank as I digested food better. The decision to stop eating wheat gave me momentum.

Then I read a chapter in *Four Hour Body*[6] that talks about losing 20 pounds in a month. It worked. I lost almost 30. More momentum. I started running around the neighborhood block. Half-miles at first. It was a far cry from a marathon, but it put me in motion. It was a small, obtainable goal.

Along with my physical health, I had neglected reading and working on my craft as a writer. I started by reading fiction, and committed myself to blogging once a month. Donald Miller asked me to write with him on his Storyline blog. So I did.

When I was depressed, my spiritual life also derailed. It felt more like something else I had to do, instead of a relationship. It felt like a duty I was failing. I tried to just get honest with God. When I did, it felt like he didn't want me to do all the religious duties. He just wanted me to love him, love others, and do stuff.

Work didn't feel so overwhelming anymore, as I found strength to put up boundaries and say no. So what if I have four-thousand unread e-mails and seventy-two voice mail messages right now? They can wait. What if I stopped worrying about pleasing others?

The momentum affected all of my life, as a man and a father. I found new intention and energy to date my wife, and no longer needed to wait for her initiation. I had new energy to love her by serving her, which is her love language. I built her planter boxes and started creating space for her to pursue urban gardening and things she loves.

Rosie and Little Bird are the shining joys of my life.

My early fears were unfounded—Something Awful was wrong. Even though I didn't know what I was doing as the father of girls, I've been loving them the best I know how. They love me, too.

These days, when I get home and walk in the door, they scream and run and ambush me, latching on to my legs. If I'm tired, I just lie on my back and they play "hop on pop." On Saturdays, we eat pancakes and watch trains. Or go to the park and swing together. Before bed, I tell them "Once Upon a Time" fairy tales. They give me hugs and kisses, and sing "Amazing Grace" with me. It's pretty much the best ever.

The mythic steps give me direction as a man, as a husband and a dad.

I hope they do the same for you.

I hope they lead you to the wild masculine, helping you find your courage and strength. I pray this book is your road map to the ManCave. Looking back, I don't think there really is a Man-Cave at all. It's more like a path.

I think manhood is more about locking arms with a small tribe of men and moving forward on the mythic path. Together. The mythic path is something we discover and walk every day. May you find the grace to walk it.

I'd love to meet you, and do my best to answer everyone I meet on Twitter.

Please feel free to say hello.

Yours sincerely,
@JohnSowers

Acknowledgments

This book is a collection of voices.

Believers, supporters, risk-takers, critics, and friends—and for these I am grateful. There are far too many to mention, but I will name a few here:

Kari, my lovely and supportive wife who worked and created space for me to write. Without you, this book would not exist. Rosie and Dassi for providing laughter and joy along the way. Don and Blair Jacobson, for believing in me as a writer and this book. You fought and paved the way for this. Blair, I deny any stories of late-night varmint hunting. Wendy Grisham and Joey Paul, thanks for taking a chance on me; I hope your faith is rewarded. You have changed me as a writer. Chelsea Apple, Laura Wheeler, Kallie Shimek, and the rest of the Hachette and Jericho crews, for your patience and edits and attention.

My mom and grandmother, for raising me, giving me a love for books, and teaching me how to write. Thanks to my brother for believing in me and giving me someone to look up to. Dad for the conversations and trip to Kodiak. Chris for your friendship and skills with a camera. My varied and sundry friends who read this and believed in it from the start: Donald Miller, who asked me to lead The Mentoring Project five years ago. Amazing ride. Bob Goff for your friendship and epic support of our wild dreams. For the Board and Staff at TMP: Jim, Kurt, Kari, Krisnee, Stephanie,

Bruce, and Marcus who believe in this message and give me freedom to write. Thanks to the folks in Portland and OKC who support us: Tom, Dewey, Jefferson, Scott, Stu, Jonathan, Chad, Rex, Ben, Jenna, Rossi, and others. A huge thank-you to all TMP mentors who are quiet heroes, and for those donors who sponsor them to mentor.

For the mentors who have poured into my life: Bill Smith, Robert Coleman, Larry Bratvold, Jim Pringle, Gail Walker, Duke Revard, Ed Eason, Jon Collins, Sonny Gault, Tom Reid, Colin James, Keith Kirk, and many others. For writers who have gone before me and paved landscapes and taught me even in your absence. I hope to meet you someday. Robert Bly, Joseph Campbell, Martin Shaw, John Eldredge, Stu Weber, Gordon Dalbey—for showing me dig sites to the wells of the wild masculine. Others who opened mythic landscapes for me, J. R. R. Tolkien, C. S. Lewis and the rest of the Inklings, George MacDonald, Paul Young, Langston Hughes, Anne LaMott, Terry Brooks, Richard Foster, Thomas Merton, Brennan Manning, and others.

Notes

Chapter One: The Murdock Files

1. Garrison Keillor, *The Book of Guys* (New York: Viking Press, 1994).

Chapter Two: Man Guides

1. Jay Z in "Jay Z Blue," YouTube video, 0:47 from Jay Z, Samsung, *Magna Carta Holy Grail*. Posted June 28, 2013 by Samsung Mobile USA.

2. Mitchell Hurwitz, *Arrested Development* (Imagine Television, 20th Century Fox, 2003–2013).

3. Barack Obama, Speech at The White House: Office of the Press Secretary, November 16, 2010.

Chapter Three: The Road Goes Ever On

1. Mary Anne Radmacher, *Courage Doesn't Always Roar* (Newburyport, MA: Conari Press, 2009).

2. James Toback, *Tyson: The Movie* (Sony Pictures Classics, 2009).

3. Ibid.

4. Ibid.

5. "The Heavyweight Muddle," *Sports Illustrated*, March 25, 1963, p. 3.

6. Lao Tzu and Stephen Mitchell, *Tao Te Ching* (New York: Harper Perennial, 1900).

Chapter Four: Woman as Salvation

1. J. R. R. Tolkien, *The Silmarillion*, 2nd Edition (New York: Mariner Press, 2001).

2. Robert Bly, *Iron John: A Book About Men* (Boston: DeCapo Press, 2004).

Chapter Five: The Wild Masculine

1. W. H. Auden, "Bucolics: Woods," recorded poem (Regis Records, 1953).

2. Robert Bly, *Iron John: A Book About Men* (Boston: DeCapo Press, 2004).

3. Martin Shaw, *A Branch from the Lightning Tree: Ecstatic Myth and the Grace of Wildness* (Ashland, OR: White Cloud Press, 2011).

4. Galway Kinnell, "Middle of the Way," from *Selected Poems* (Boston: Houghton Mifflin, 1982).

Chapter Six: The Mythic Path

1. Henry David Thoreau, *Walden* (Greensboro, NC: Empire Books, 2013).

2. Rumi, "Unfold Your Own Myth," in Roger Housden, *Ten Poems to Set You Free* (New York: Harmony Books, 2003).

3. J. R. R. Tolkien, *Tree and Leaf* (New York: Houghton Mifflin, 1965). An expanded version of the conversation between Lewis and Tolkien can be found in Humphrey Carpenter, *The Inklings* (New York: Houghton Mifflin, 1979).

4. J. R. R. Tolkien, "On Fairy Stories," in *Tree and Leaf*.

5. Ludwig von Beethoven, July 1814, Baden, after benefit performance of "Fidelio," in *Beethoven: The Man and the Artist, as Revealed in His Own Words*, Friedrich Kerst and Henry Edward Krehbiel, eds., public domain.

6. Saint Augustine, *Exposition on the Book of Psalms*, Psalm 133, expos. no. 6, in *Nicene and Post-Nicene Fathers*, series 1, vol. 8, public domain.

7. Maurice Sendak, *Where the Wild Things Are* (New York: HarperCollins, 1962).

Chapter Seven: Movimentio Es Vida

1. Timothy Ferriss, *Four Hour Body: An Unusual Guide to Rapid Fat Loss, Incredible Sex and Becoming Superhuman* (New York: Harmony Books, 2010).

2. Max Brooks, *World War Z* (Paramount Pictures, 2013).

3. Joyce Carol Oates, "Mike Tyson," in *Iron Mike*, Daniel O'Connor, ed. (New York: Thunder's Mouth Press, 2002), italics added.

4. Stephen Pressfield, *The War of Art, Break Through the Blocks and Win Your Inner Creative Battles* (New York: Black Irish Entertainment, 2012).

5. Eden Phillpotts, *The Shadow Passes* (New York: Macmillan, 1919).

6. Jack London, *The Call of the Wild* (New York: Macmillan, 1903)

7. Charles Duhigg, *The Power of Habit* (New York: Random House, 2012)

8. W. H. Murray, *The Scottish Himalayan Expedition* (London: J. M. Dent and Co., 1954).

Chapter Eight: Into the Red Earth

1. J. R. R. Tolkien, *The Lord of the Rings* (New York: Houghton Mifflin, 1967).

2. MuteMath, "OK," from *Reset* (Warner Music Group, 2004).

3. Thomas Merton, *The Hidden Ground of Love: The Letters of Thomas Merton on Religious Experience and Social Concerns* (New York: Harcourt Brace, 1983).

4. Martin Shaw, *A Branch from the Lightning Tree: Ecstatic Myth and the Grace of Wildness* (Ashland, OR: White Cloud Press, 2011).

Chapter Nine: The River

1. Marquis de Lafayette, "Speech to the Constituent Assembly," 1790.

2. C. S. Lewis, *Reflections on the Psalms* (New York: Mariner Books, 1964).

Chapter Ten: The Resistance

1. Renzo Gracie (Renzo_Gracie_BJJ), "Fighting is the best thing a man can have in his soul." October 8, 2012, 8:53 a.m. Tweet.

2. Jack Dempsey, *Championship Fighting: Explosive Punching and Aggressive Defense* (New York: Prentice Hall, 1950).

3. Bruce Lee, *Tao of Jeet Kun Do* (South Bend, IN: Ohara Publications, 1975).

4. Thomas Merton, *New Seeds of Contemplation* (New York: New Directions, 2007).

5. Martin Luther, as quoted in Vincent Cronin, *The Flowering of the Renaissance* (New York: HarperCollins, 1969).

6. Thomas Jefferson, "Thomas Jefferson Retirement Papers," 1834.

Chapter Eleven: A Living Flame

1. Martin Shaw, *A Branch from the Lightning Tree: Ecstatic Myth and the Grace of Wildness* (Ashland, OR: White Cloud Press, 2011).

2. Richard Foster, *Prayer: Finding the Heart's True Home* (New York, HarperOne, 1992).

3. Andrew Bonar, *Memoir and Remains of Robert Murray M'Cheyne* (Edinburg: William Oliphant and Co., 1862).

4. John G. Neihardt, *Black Elk Speaks* (Albany, NY: State University of New York Press, 2008).

5. C. S. Lewis, *Mere Christianity* (New York: Macmillan, 1952).

6. Tom Shippey gives an excellent explanation of Tolkien's invention and use of the term "Eucatastrophe" in *The Return of the King* DVD commentary (New Line Cinema, 2003).

7. J. R. R. Tolkien, *The Return of the King* (London: George Allen and Unwin, 1955).

8. Ibid.

Chapter Twelve: There and Back Again

1. Sir Thomas Carlyle, *On Heroes, Hero Worship and the Heroic in History* (London: James Fraser, 1841).
2. Kiser, John, *The Monks of Tibhirine: Faith, Love, and Terror in Algeria* (New York: St. Martin's Griffin, 2003).
3. Ibid.
4. C. S. Lewis, *Mere Christianity* (New York: Macmillan, 1952).
5. Imagine Dragons, "Radioactive," from *Night Visions* (Interscope, 2012).
6. Timothy Ferriss, *Four Hour Body: An Unusual Guide to Rapid Fat Loss, Incredible Sex and Becoming Superhuman* (New York: Harmony Books, 2010).

About the Author

JOHN SOWERS is the President of The Mentoring Project, a movement rewriting the fatherless story through mentoring. His work has been featured by CNN, Fox News, *Christianity Today*, and *RELEVANT*, and he received the President's Champion of Change Award at the White House. John loves his family, small-batch coffee, bow hunting, and the Boston Red Sox.